STRENGTH
IN NUMBERS

TURNING WORK GROUPS
INTO TEAMS

STRENGTH

I N   N U M B E R S

Leslie Bendaly

McGraw-Hill Ryerson
Montreal   Toronto

To My Team at Home —
Elie, Nicole and Chip

First published in 1990 by
McGraw-Hill Ryerson Limited
330 Progress Avenue
Toronto, Canada
M1P 2Z5

Second Printing 1991

Canadian Cataloguing in Publication Data

Bendaly, Leslie
  Strength in numbers: turning work groups into teams

ISBN 0-07-551023-5

1. Work groups. 2. Organizational effectiveness.
3. Management. I. Title.

HD66.B45 1990   658.4′036   C90-094183-9

 Printed and bound in Canada using acid-free paper.

2 3 4 5 6 7 8 9 10   AP   9 8 7 6 5 4 3 2 1

Contents

Preface

It is time to focus and simplify.

The past decade has been a busy one for managers. In our frantic search for excellence, we have attempted to be cultural heroes, participative managers, team leaders, change agents, mentors, and visionaries. We have Managed by Walking Around, implemented Quality Circles and other employee-involvement programs, identified values and beliefs, developed mission and philosophy statements, focused on the customer and quality, championed innovation, fostered ownership and entrepreneurism and, with any time left over, empowered our employees.

Many, however, were so busy searching for the newest and best road to excellence, or for "eureka," as one manager put it when asked what she was looking for, that not enough effort was effectively and consistently applied. Activity became the measure of success. Glossy and slick programs were implemented to support one new management value or approach after another. Too often, they become appendages to the organization, rather than tools for weaving the value or approach into the organizational fiber. Organizations labored over mission and philosophy statements, but frequently more effort was put into wordsmithing than into operationalizing them.

In spite of this, gains were made. Most organizations are somewhere on the path toward a more effective, participative, and flexible organization. Results, however, were less dramatic and strides shorter than we had originally anticipated.

Happily there are organizations that have reaped considerable rewards. They recognized the need to focus on participation and teamwork and, through persistence, an understanding of the tools and techniques, and a systematic approach, they have experienced exciting results.

Indeed, most organizations do an enormous number of things correctly. When I do team development work, I frequently meet groups that are doing almost everything "right." They may be missing only one or two small pieces of the teamwork puzzle. They may actually hold the missing piece in their hands and have forgotten it is there, or they may not know how or where to place it. The impetus for this book, then, is not that "so many managers are doing so many things wrong," but that "so many committed people are doing so many things right."

Leaders recognize that in today's fast-paced, high-change organizational environments, only the fittest survive. This is true not only of individuals but of teams as well. Certainly, only the fittest teams can support their organizations in successfully facing today's numerous and complex challenges. I believe that in North America our organizational Achilles' heel is our tendency not to apply what we already know. My purpose in writing this book is not to provide you with more theory and general information which you may or may not ever find the time to turn into action. It is to share with you the critical success elements of fit and thriving teams and to provide you with easy steps for making them part of your team. Some of you will be looking for a management overview of teamwork essentials, others who are facilitating teams and want to apply the information immediately will also be looking for specific tools.

With this in mind, I have divided this book into sections addressing each of the key elements of a fit team: productive participation, openness, cohesiveness, and change compatibility. I have also included a section addressing other critical and current teamwork issues: leadership, self-managed work teams, and committees. Finally, I have added a chapter responding to the most common "how-to" questions. Those readers looking for specific techniques will find them at the end of each section under the Workouts.

Instruments to support the maintenance of fit teams are described in the final section: "Team Fitness: Maintaining the Momentum."

It is not difficult to increase teamwork effectiveness dramatically, but it requires knowledge, tools, commitment, and action.

The chapters that follow are intended to provide you with the knowledge and tools to facilitate action and to spark renewed commitment in any of you who may need reenergizing.

Leslie Bendaly

The Team Fitness Elements

1

Team Fitness

Getting Beyond Survival

Survival depends on balance. If an organization is to thrive, its balancing act must be fine tuned because today's organization is buffeted by innumerable challenges. We face changes that are unprecedented in both pace and magnitude. Frequent changes used to be considered a symptom of ineffective management. Now if an organization does not change often enough, quickly enough, and effectively enough, it won't survive. Technology, the economy, global competition, and new social trends have produced an array of changes that can be and indeed have been devastating to many organizations. Most are coping with one or several of the more common changes: new technologies, organizational restructuring, new corporate strategies, new product lines or enhancements, tighter budget controls, and higher employee expectations. In addition, organizations must manage externally imposed changes such as new government regulations. The number and diversity of changes experienced simultaneously frequently overload an organization's system and its people. Employees, who may have accepted an occasional change implemented slowly, are not as ready to welcome sudden, quickly implemented, and often drastic change. Systems that were designed to manage and maintain the status quo are inadequate in an environment of accelerated change that calls for quick corporate reflexes.

In addition, we are in an age of transition between the traditional hierarchical organization and the participative team-oriented one. Each organization is at a different place on the transitional path, but all are faced with similar challenges. The limiting yet protective boxes into which each person fits in a traditional organization are being broken down. Roles and expectations are being reevaluated. The process of transition requires resilience, flexibility, and a good deal of insight. We must identify which aspects of the former organization are still valid and should be maintained and which require replacement. Seasoned managers must shed old management behaviors which served them well in the past and adopt new and sometimes initially uncomfortable management methods. Employees conditioned to be task oriented must strive to become innovative problem-solvers. We must all learn the techniques that make participation work.

Balancing, always a good management idea, is now critical. We must achieve and maintain the balance between

effectiveness & efficiency
quality & cost
task & process
change & status quo
leadership & management.

In order to achieve that balance, an organization must be fit. The fitness of the organization depends upon the fitness of the many teams that support it. Teams at peak fitness may seem too good to be true. They have the resilience to bounce back when knocked down, the dexterity to avoid pitfalls and to juggle apparently contradictory objectives, the flexibility to change gears and direction suddenly, the ability to deal with the unexpected, the quick reflexes to duck when the not-so-good stuff hits the fan, the commitment to keep going when the going gets tough, and the endurance to succeed. More simply, they thrive in competitive and unpredictable environments.

As individuals, we have recognized the relationship between fitness and success. The fitness craze of the eighties has become a way of life for us. We jog, walk, run, play racquet sports, ride bikes, and swim to develop a toned and optimally functioning body that can excel in spite of stressful environments. Toned and fit teams are also the result of a concerted and consistent effort. Teams must periodically check their fitness level, recognize areas that need developing, and put themselves through the appropriate workouts to achieve the desired degree of fitness. They must also ensure that they have a maintenance program in place to keep them where they want to be. This is not necessarily a time-consuming process, but it does require vigilance and consistency.

Teams fall predominantly into one of three organizational fitness categories: rigid, limp, or flexible.

The Rigid Group

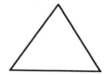

Rigid groups are run by policies and procedures, and although group members may complain about the number of rules, they complain just as loudly if a guideline is not in place for a specific task. Members also complain about how things are done, but when new procedures are introduced, the old methods suddenly look pretty good. Rigid groups tend to be task rather than process oriented and can be recognized by statements such as: "That's not the way it's done here"; "That'll never work. We tried that a couple of years ago"; "We've always done it that way"; "If it ain't broke, why fix it?"; and "I don't know. You're the boss."

The manager is the hub of the department and is expected to have all answers to all questions; to make decisions, since the department believes that that is what she's paid to do; to interpret tasks; to establish priorities; and in general, to control everything. The leader is quite happy to try to fulfill these expectations as they basically describe a definition of management with which she is comfortable. The leader is an authority figure and sees her role as distinct from the team and set apart from them. She spends most of her time away from the team in her own office, at her own desk, and at meetings. If she needs to make contact, she usually calls a team member in to her. When she does appear among the group, her purpose is usually

to make an announcement. If asked to identify the most important aspect of a manager's role, she would likely respond "to
control."

In the rigid team, meetings are infrequent, are seen generally as a waste of time, and are run by the manager who uses
them for the most part to communicate information and plans.
Other than "for clarification" — questions related to information conveyed by the manager — communication is for the most
part one way.

When faced with change, the rigid team often simply deflects
it through resistance. If the change is imposed and therefore
must happen, implementation is usually difficult. The group is
frequently damaged by its inability to adapt, and the expected
benefits of the change are seldom realized.

The Limp Group

The limp group has a very different personality. Policies and
procedures are ignored as much as possible under the guise
of greater efficiency or with the comment that rules are made
to be broken. Why waste time, a limp group would argue, when
we can get to the same place by a shorter route? The incom-
pleteness or inconsistency of the shorter route, however, often
creates problems for the group or for other groups who depend
upon its work.

Limp groups can be recognized by such statements as: "We're
all one big happy family"; "Let's not sweat the small stuff";
"Who's getting the coffee and donuts for the meeting?"; "We
want to make sure everybody feels good about this"; "Whatever happened to that idea we had?"

When faced with change, the limp group usually does not
overtly resist it, because being positive and agreeable are strong
group norms. However, neither does it embrace change, and
so change may seem to be implemented deceivingly easily,
but then not take.

The limp manager sees himself as a motivator and is definitely a carrot man. Keeping his people happy is his number one priority. He believes that if people are happy, the job will get done. He is frequently disappointed, but usually finds a reason for the failure somewhere in his human relations philosophy: "We didn't keep John sufficiently informed"; "I should have checked out how Sally felt"; or "Ken's been having a hard time at home." He refers to the group as "my people" or "my team." He is usually very visible, and he makes regular forays out into the group. The resulting interactions are usually personal in nature: "Hi, how are you? How are the children?"

The group tends to be more process oriented than task oriented. Meetings are frequent and usually chaired by a manager who wants to "check how you're all feeling about this." He asks, "What do you feel about this? I want your input," but it is not unusual for him then to try enthusiastically to sell the group on the decision he has already made. The limp group's desire to be one big happy family, and so be positive and agreeable, pervades, and members usually support the manager's idea, at least until they leave the meeting room.

Consensus is important to the group, but so is being sensitive to each other. In group decision-making and problem-solving sessions, ideas are discussed and rediscussed in an effort to find a middle-of-the-road compromise that everyone finds acceptable, and no one finds offensive. The decision made is usually not the decision that would most positively impact on performance but the one that keeps most people happy. Results are inefficient and ineffective. Everyone goes away half-happy, and no one leaves with the enthusiasm to carry the idea forward with energy.

Although members often discuss at length upcoming changes, most decisions in limp groups are ultimately made by the manager. In some cases, this manager involves people primarily to make them feel good; he may not be ready to share the decision-making process sincerely. In other instances, however, the manager makes the decision out of frustration because he and the group do not have the skills to manage the group decision-making process.

Although the rigid group and the limp group work very differently and have very different personalities, they both have much in common and can both usually be described to varying degrees as lethargic, uncommitted, discordant, and dysfunctional. They are both in a self-destruct mode, yet they seldom recognize this. They see their state of ineffectiveness as being caused by "them" or "it," which encompass any factors outside of their control, including upper management, government, competitors, the economy, and so on.

Limp, however, can be the more dangerous mode because it is deceptive. The manager believes he is a team leader and that he has a team. Group members frequently believe that they are a team. On the surface, many of their activities, including meetings and social events, may reinforce this belief. As a result, the group does not recognize why it is not achieving its potential.

The Flexible Team

The fit team is flexible and energized. It stands out in its ability to respond and adapt quickly and with ease to internal and external changes and pressures. It has the endurance to handle most marathons, the high energy for sprints, and the resilience to bounce back when bombarded with the unexpected.

The leader of the flexible team sees herself as a team member, leader, and facilitator. She feels no need to motivate her team members, and carries neither carrots nor sticks. Instead, she provides challenges, opportunities, and resources. Members of fit and flexible teams have many common denominators:

- They believe they are not only responsible for their own job, but also share the responsibility for the team's results.
- They enjoy their work.
- They feel a sense of accomplishment.

- They generally look forward to coming to work.
- They consistently give more than required.
- They respect and trust their fellow team members.
- They demonstrate well-honed group skills.
- They are productive.
- They are proactive.

Team members leave their regular meetings exhilarated and enthusiastic, with a feeling of accomplishment. The flexible group consistently reaches and surpasses targets in spite of obstacles. It is made up of individuals who have many individual differences, and yet can form a cohesive unit.

The flexible group can be recognized by statements such as: "We may not like it, but we are going to do our damnedest to make it work"; "I don't think the rest of you understood my point. Can I try again?"; "Yes, there are some negative outside factors, but what can *we* do to improve things?"; "I don't think we're aiming high enough on that one"; "I'm not sure I handled that as well as I could have. I'd appreciate some input from the rest of you." The fit team uses its energy positively; has open, confident communication among its members; sees critiquing as essential to growth; and does not find a scapegoat for why things go wrong, but takes responsibility for making things work.

Although most organizations recognize the need for teamwork and are increasing their flexibility, those teams that have met their optimum level of fitness are still the exception, not the norm. The success of our organizations and ultimately our economy rests on our ability to manage and to thrive on change. The essential ingredient for success is a team sufficiently fit to meet the challenge.

How Fit Is Your Team?

Like individuals, each team is unique. Each has its own fitness profile, depending upon the strengths and mix of four critical

Rigid Group

Symbols
Based on the traditional organizational pyramid representing top-down decision-making, very firm lines, no flexibility.

Limp Group

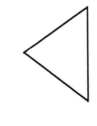

The circle at the bottom represents process and participation. The circle is not closed however, because process is generally incomplete, and closure and action often do not occur. The wavy lines represent limpness, and the point at the top suggests that in most cases the decision-maker is still the most senior person.

Flexible Team

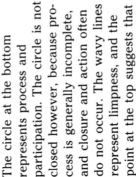

The closed circles represent productive participation throughout the organization, in different directions, involving different people in different issues at different times. The variety of circles and directions suggests flexibility. The solid lines, however, suggest structure and guidelines. This is not a participative free-for-all. The circle at the top represents participative decision-making.

Foundation	Based on policies and procedures, rules and regulations. People at the top make the decision.	Based on interpersonal relationships; appears to involve people, but management still makes most of the decisions.	Based on effective teamwork and productive employee participation. Decision-making is shared whenever appropriate.
Assumption	Assumption: The job will get done if employees are controlled.	Assumption: If people are happy the job will get done.	Assumption: If people participate productively,* the job will be done well. An additional benefit is that people will be "happy."
Response to Change	Change is deflected. When it is forced to penetrate, it does damage to the group, and the group consciously or unconsciously sabotages it. Expected results are seldom achieved.	Change is usually accepted, but not integrated and seldom takes. Expected results are often not achieved.	Change is readily assimilated and expected results are consistently realized.

*What we mean by participating productively is described in the section entitled "Productive Participation," p. 24.

team characteristics. Groups that achieve the desired balance and consistently realize their potential have several common denominators. They are cohesive, open, ensure the productive participation of all members, have well-developed group skills, and manage change effectively. The extent to which each of these is present determines the fitness level of the group and marks the difference between a group and a team. Both the traditional group, with a formal leader — perhaps a manager, supervisor, or chairperson — and the more modern leaderless team can be assessed by the degree to which each of these elements is evident.

In each structure, if functioning optimally, all members are responsible for the fitness level of the group, but in the more traditional group the qualities of the leader determine to a great extent the strength of each of the elements. We will examine the leadership role later.

Team Element 1:
Productive Participation

Participation is essential if a group is to be a team. Without participation, members have little sense of ownership, and without ownership, commitment is unlikely. In fit teams, members have an opportunity to be involved at some level in changes that affect them. They view participation not merely as an opportunity, but as a responsibility. Consequently, the process of participation is effective and efficient and the outcome is beneficial. If productive participation is to happen, the leader must involve people for the right reasons; the right people must be involved at the right time in the right issues; and participants must clearly understand their roles.

Group skills are also essential to productive participation. These include facilitating, meeting, problem-solving and decision-making skills. When group skills are weak, members frequently have a sense of frustration. They feel that much time is spent in discussions and in meetings and yet little is accomplished. Often they are confused about what has been decided or resent decisions that did not go the preferred way.

I was once asked to sit in on a meeting of an employee-involvement committee. The committee's mandate was to identify opportunities for involving frontline people in decisions that had traditionally been management's territory. The committee consisted of nine representatives. The facilitator, Susan, opened the meeting well, recapping decisions from the previous meeting and updating members on actions taken.

"Actions taken on the decision to post the minutes of our meeting include posting minutes of the last meeting in the library and sending out a memo this morning to let everyone know they are there," Susan began.

The immediate response from three of the nine members was, "What? I thought we had decided *not* to post the minutes."

Susan was startled and somewhat embarrassed. She later acknowledged, however, that the incident had been beneficial in that it had forced the group to look at its facilitation and decision-making skills. By concentrating on these areas, the committee measurably increased its productivity and effectiveness. We will examine this group more closely in Chapter 3.

The following types of comments reflect the need for strengthening group skills: "We've met on that three times already, and we still can't come to an agreement"; "Not another meeting!"; "We made a decision all right, but I'm not sure it's the best"; "Only a few of us are participating"; "Whatever happened to that idea we had last month?"

Productive participation includes involving the right people in the right issues at the right time and strong group skills to ensure the process is effective and efficient.

Team Element 2:
Openness

I once worked with a group that had two team members who worked side by side and had not spoken to each other for fifteen years. Uncooperative relationships within the group were accepted as the norm, and trust and openness were nonexistent. Not all groups that lack openness are as obviously dysfunctional as this one. However, team members are acutely aware when this element is lacking. The tension is felt by individual members and is manifested by the team in weakened vital signs.

Openness is the foundation for all teamwork. If open and honest communication and trust are lacking, little room for growth remains. When people can't give each other input, they can't learn from each other; when people can't express their true feelings, conflicts aren't managed; when people are hesitant to communicate openly within the group, they can't come to agreement on goals and work values, and cohesiveness can't exist; when people can't be honest, true consensus can't be reached. Cohesiveness is impossible without openness.

In a limp group, team members frequently feign comfort and agreement in an attempt to fulfill the expectation that the team is "one big happy family." In this dysfunctional style, employees run to the manager, who plays the role of mom or dad, to resolve disputes. They are unable to be sufficiently open with one another to manage personal conflicts.

In the rigid group, the hostility and distrust are often evident. Less effort is made to feign comfort and agreement. In some sense, more honesty exists in this group, but it is equally dysfunctional because the members are not sufficiently open to prevent and resolve conflicts. Members are not likely to "run to" the rigid manager with conflict problems, and he doesn't see "keeping people happy" as his priority. As a result, conflicts are often ignored and become entrenched in the group as did the behavior of the workmates who hadn't spoken for fifteen years.

The lack of openness may derive from a culture that dictates that openness is not "the way we do things around here" or from a lack of skills in giving and receiving feedback. This lack of openness, trust, and constructive feedback means that team members' opportunity for growth is limited, as is their opportunity for sharing problem-solving and decision-making on task-related issues.

When openness is lacking, communication between team members focuses on social conversation. Work-related discussion is often negative in nature and lacks constructive sharing of information or problem-solving.

Team Element 3:
Cohesiveness

"Cohesive" is the most common response I receive when I ask people to describe an ideal team. When I ask what they mean by cohesive, they usually respond "sticking together." People instinctively know that cohesiveness is an important team element, and they feel the loss when it is not there. Usually, however, they don't know what glue they need in order to "stick together" more effectively.

That glue has two primary ingredients:

- Agreement with the mandate, goals, and objectives of the team (*what* the team is there to do);
- Agreement with the work values and culture of the team (*how* the team functions).

I think of the mandate, goals, and objectives as the body of teamwork. These elements are usually clear cut and so relatively easy to define and agree to. More elusive, however, and yet vital to the health of the body is the soul or spirit. I think of the teamwork values as the spirit. The values which are demonstrated create the team culture.

Yet values are more nebulous than goals and objectives and, therefore, often more difficult to identify and agree upon.

Since the need to have a vision and to develop organizational cultures has been recognized, teams are somewhat more comfortable working with the concept of values. Many can list their organizational values. They often have a more difficult time, however, identifying values that pertain specifically to their own team as opposed to the entire organization.

When members of a team *are* able to identify commonly held values, they will frequently express them in motherhood kinds of statements. Who is going to say, "No, I don't agree with quality customer service"? The tough part is to get agreement in action. This requires relatively consistent demonstration of that value by each team member. When this doesn't happen, conflict arises. Lack of agreement on work values and the demonstration of those values is the most common source of conflict within work groups. When one team member interprets "quality customer service" as picking up the phone on the first ring and another member interprets it as picking up the phone on the fifth ring, we have the potential for conflict.

Nonagreement on work values can be a major impediment to doing a job well. When cohesiveness is weak, we don't have a team but a group of people each going in his or her own direction.

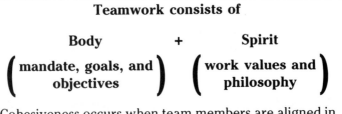

Teamwork consists of

Body + **Spirit**

$\left(\begin{array}{c}\text{mandate, goals, and}\\\text{objectives}\end{array}\right)$ $\left(\begin{array}{c}\text{work values and}\\\text{philosophy}\end{array}\right)$

Cohesiveness occurs when team members are aligned in both.

Team Element 4:
Change Compatibility

Organizational life has been irreparably altered. As the pace of change accelerates, the organization in which maintaining the status quo is the norm and change the exception is fast fading from corporate memory. The team that thrives today must be able to maintain its high performance in an environment of accelerated and successive changes. Change compatibility requires receptivity to change, adaptability to change, effective evaluation of opportunities for change, and the assimilation of change. When these characteristics exist in a team, change is seen not as a threat, but an opportunity. Change is not a burden but a challenge. The team is not simple surviving, but is thriving.

The Quickest Route to Team Fitness

Exasperated team members and team leaders often ask, "Why is it so hard for people to work together as a team?" To the contrary, I find it amazing that groups work together as well as they do. People are hired for their technical or professional skills and not for their team skills. They are given a job description and probably a manual of procedures, a desk, cubicle, territory, or office and are usually told that the reward system is based on personal job performance. We ask people to come out of their cubicles for a weekly, monthly, or perhaps only annual team meeting and then wonder why they can't work together cooperatively. But people cannot be expected to work together effectively if they are seldom put into a situation where they are required to do so. Although teams are essential for high performance, many organizations "scrape by" on individual performance.

Imagine hiring a group of skilled athletes, asking each to practice his own skills independently, giving each a manual of rules to read, and then putting them together on a field only at the moment of the first game. This group, of course, would not function as a team any more than do the individuals we put together in an organization.

In order to develop as a team, a group must come together periodically to examine its effectiveness and practice working as a team. The more regularly and productively the team meets, the quicker it develops. *Productively* is, of course, the key word here. Some groups feel they are developing as teams simply because they meet together regularly. Simply coming together does not develop a team. What happens when the group comes together must be planned and productive.

Team development occurs when a team pauses to examine itself, identifies opportunities for improvement, and agrees to them, with commitment to action.

It is possible to enhance team performance without taking a team through a fitness-development process. The results, however, are less dramatic and much more slowly realized. Teams can't truly realize their potential without accepting ownership for their own team development. The ideal, however, of coming together regularly for team-development purposes is not always possible. Some leaders cannot get all team members together on a regular basis; others may not be ready to do so.

We can make some impact on team fitness by a less formal method of team development which we refer to as the backdoor method. The leader does not announce team development, but sets about consistently strengthening team elements in a less direct manner. In particular, the leader assesses his own style and consistently works at developing the four dimensions of team leadership described in the leadership section, page 135. In addition, he uses tools and techniques to develop specific elements, such as cohesiveness or openness, as the opportunity arises.

Whether you use the quicker, more dramatic route of taking your team through fitness workouts or you choose the backdoor method, the information and tools in the following pages will support you in enhancing your team's performance.

Team Workout for Increasing Team Fitness

Workout: To assist you in assessing your team's strength in each of the four critical fitness elements.

Steps:
1. Request team members to complete the following Team Fitness Test anonymously and submit the Team Fitness Scoring Sheet.
2. Compile data from the scoring sheets using the Team Fitness Interpretation sheet.
3. Share output from the fitness test with the team and in the process examine both team strengths and opportunities for improvement.
4. Develop strategies for improvement.
5. Make specific commitments to action.

Team Fitness Test

Read each of the following statements with your team in mind. Rate each of the statements as it applies to your team using the following scale:

1 This statement is never true of our team.
2 This statement is occasionally true of our team.
3 This statement applies to our team most of the time.
4 This statement always applies to our team.

Enter the score you believe appropriate for each statement beside the statement number on the Scoring Sheet.

1. Team members have an opportunity to be involved in decisions that affect them.
2. Team members know they can depend on each other.
3. Team members understand and agree on our mandate, goals, and objectives.
4. Our team is open to new ideas.
5. We leave our meetings with a sense of accomplishment.
6. There is a feeling of trust in our team.
7. Our expectations of each other are periodically clarified.
8. Once a change is implemented in our team, it sticks.
9. Team members' suggestions and ideas are used whenever possible.
10. Team members do not allow personal priorities or hidden agendas to hinder team effectiveness.
11. Our roles are clearly defined and accepted as defined by all team members.
12. We take a positive attitude toward change with which we may not agree but over which we have no control.
13. The time team members devote to participation in meetings, committees, or task forces is well used.
14. Team members feel free to give their honest opinions.

15. If we were each asked to list departmental/team priorities, our lists would be very similar.
16. We are receptive to change, but do not get caught up in "change for the sake of change."
17. When sharing a decision, we usually come to a consensus easily.
18. Team members respect each other.
19. Team members hold similar work values.
20. Our team implements change effectively.

Team Effectiveness Scoring Sheet

I		II		III		IV	
Statement	Score	Statement	Score	Statement	Score	Statement	Score
1		2		3		4	
5		6		7		8	
9		10		11		12	
13		14		15		16	
17		18		19		20	
Total		Total		Total		Total	

Transfer your totals to the following interpretation grid.

Team Fitness Interpretation

Column	Your Score	Priority	Team Average	Team Priority	Team Element
I					Productive Participation
II					Openness
III					Cohesiveness
IV					Change Compatibility

Your lowest score will be ranked number1; second lowest score number 2; and so on. This identifies the elements that require development in an order of priority from 1 to 4.

The Team Average is used when team members are invited to evaluate their team's fitness. It is obtained simply by totaling the individual scores for each element and dividing by the number of members who have completed the fitness test.

The Team Priority column results from ranking the team averages. This not only identifies strengths, weaknesses, and priority items, but gives individual team members the opportunity to compare their view of the team with the general team view. It can be particularly useful for a team leader to compare his view of the team with that of team members.

Team Fitness Element 1
PRODUCTIVE
PARTICIPATION

2

Experiencing Participation at Its Best

The Potential Perils of Participation

Most managers, if not already committed to teamwork and participation, have made forays into the participative world. Participation has been hard to resist since for many years it was sold with great hype and fanfare, almost as an elixir. We were told it could cure almost any organizational ache, whether inadequacies in quality, productivity, or morale. It seemed an easy-enough treatment to apply: ask people for their input. As a result, some managers didn't read the instructions and others applied it without really believing in it or understanding the principle. Since it seemed innocuous, many applied it without a great deal of attention to how it was applied. They found that the aches didn't go away. In fact, some new ones appeared. Some managers began to suspect the elixir was really snake oil and retreated to their perhaps imperfect, but familiar rigid or limp methods.

When we find participation does not live up to our expectations, the problem is usually rooted in at least one of three possible causes. We may not be paying enough attention to detail; people may not be involved appropriately; and in some instances, management may misunderstand the principle or not believe in it sufficiently. In these instances, participation is present but not productive.

Examples of Employee Reactions to Nonproductive Participation

Ron (Marketing Manager)
"We involve people a lot and in important matters. But

sometimes it seems like we're reinventing the wheel, not being productive. A department may already have the information or skills needed to get a particular decision made or something implemented, but we set up a task force of people and they start from scratch, do research, develop some skills, and take months to get something done that could have been done in a couple of weeks."

Burt (Line Supervisor)
"We're so committed to getting everyone's input and really listening to it and getting consensus that we seldom end up with the best decision for the organization, but instead something that will keep most of the people happy. Too often participation fulfills many managers' worst participative nightmares — that is, participation for participation's sake and the most popular rather than the best decisions."

Kathy (Frontline Clerk)
"They keep asking our opinion in meetings, but it never goes the way we want it to. If they already have their minds made up, why ask us?"

Margaret (Health Care Worker)
"We are involved in decisions in our facility, but it seems nothing ever gets implemented. We think we've made a decision and then someone says, 'I disagree,' and we rework it again. It's a case of constantly going back to the drawing board."

The organizational scenarios vary, but the frustration, disillusionment and, not infrequently, anger are the same.

Clarifying the Rules of the Game

With participation, a detail often overlooked is an explanation of the rules. Imagine spending an evening with friends and having the host announce that he has just bought a new, expensive, and very popular game called Participation. He wants everyone to play. When someone asks the objective, he responds, "To increase the quality of our evening together." Someone else asks, "How do you play it?" and he answers, "I've got a bunch of cards here with different problems that require solutions. I'll choose a card and you are to come up with ideas for a solution."

I doubt that anyone would be too excited about playing the game. The host's comments provided little incentive. "What's in it for me or us? How do I win or we win?" wasn't explained. However, since it's the host's idea, the group agrees to give it a try.

The first card pulled by the host says that a decision must be made on the purchase of a car. The players are provided with information on three makes and models of cars, including specifications, features, costs, and an automobile association's rating on performance. After a lengthy, involved, and sometimes heated discussion to which the various players bring their personal knowledge and experience about the three cars, seven out of ten group members choose car A. The host who is leading the group says, "Thanks, folks. That was a good discussion. We're going to go with car C."

The players are confused, frustrated, even angry. Inevitably, they protest, "What? I thought we had consensus."

"Doesn't the majority rule?"

"What's the point of asking our opinion if one person makes the decision anyway?"

"That was a real waste of time."

Imagine the reaction to the host's invitation to play another round?

Employees who believe that they are experiencing token participation can identify with the players and can easily see the analogy between this scenario and what is happening in their workplace. Leaders, however, who are introducing employee-involvement initiatives see the scenario quite differently. They are more liable to identify with the host, who is likely to feel some frustration himself.

"I bought this new expensive game because I thought they would like it and nobody appreciated it at all. In fact, most of them complained. I don't know why they were so upset. I said I would ask them to discuss topics. I never told them they could make the decisions."

In this scenario, the missing element was a clarification of the rules of the game. The result was differing expectations. Invitations to participate, then, need to include a clarification to prevent confusion and unrealistic expectations. When being asked for input, participants need to know how it will be used and to what extent it will influence a decision. If being asked to participate in a decision-making process, participants' roles and influencing power need to be clarified.

Clarification of the broader picture of what participative management is and why it is used may be necessary when working with groups who have little experience with it. When understanding is assumed, misbeliefs are often established.

Misbelief **A**   Participative management = Democratic rule

Misbelief **B**   Participative management is designed to keep most of the people happy

Misbelief **C**   Participative management means everyone has the right to be involved in everything

---

Once any of these misbeliefs become operational, the manager frequently feels she's damned if she does and damned if she doesn't. People are upset if the manager doesn't ask for their opinion and equally upset if she does but doesn't follow their advice. Managers don't fall into this trap when they make clear to everyone *that productive participation is involving people appropriately in organizational decision-making whenever possible to ensure decisions that best enhance the organization's well being.*

An understanding of this definition serves to dispel the misbeliefs that lead to unrealistic and therefore unfulfilled expectations. The definition focuses on increased organizational effectiveness and emphasizes the intent to involve the right people at the right time for the purpose of making better decisions for the organization or team.

Levels of Participation

Put simply, involving people appropriately means involving the right people at the right time. If, however, employees do not understand the criteria for involvement or how their opinions will be used, the actions of even the most well-intentioned participative managers will inevitably be viewed negatively.

I remember the manager of a lab who decided that he wanted his department to be more participative. He and his supervisors made a consistent effort over a six-month period to solicit opinions on decisions that would affect the staff. By the sixth month, employees were frustrated and morale had dropped. Management felt equally frustrated and had come to the conclusion that when it comes to participation, you cannot win.

Staff members were particularly angry that so many decisions did not go "their way" after they had spent considerable time giving their input. It was a revelation to the group to learn that in participative management, an invitation to participate is not necessarily an invitation to make the decision; that, in fact, many levels of participation exist, each of which is appropriate in particular circumstances. Their unrealistic expectations arose because no one had explained specifically how their input would be used or at which level they were being invited to participate.

Four levels of participation exist, each legitimate in particular circumstances. Which you choose depends upon many criteria, but the essentials are: the participant's skills and knowledge; the experience the participant brings to the decision; the extent to which the pending decision will affect him or her.

Levels of Participation

Level I   Making the decision

Level II   Sharing the decision-making (consensus)

Level III   Contributing to the collection of data being used to make the decision

Level IV   Problem solving/discussion of how to make an imposed decision work and/or if seen as a negative change, how to cope with it.

In most organizations, some decisions must be imposed. However, in a participative culture, managers are continuously and consistently preparing employees for more frequent involvement at the higher levels of participation.

The more teams function at Level I, the more they move toward self-management.

Level I Making the Decision

In the simplest terms, the manager is saying in this instance, "You know best. You make the decision." This is the ultimate level of participation and the level toward which dedicated leaders are constantly developing their people. Managers give people more decision-making authority as the combination of their skills, experience, and the situation warrants. But other levels of participation exist that are just as valid and credible to the participative philosophy.

Level II Sharing the Decision-Making

At this level, the decision is made by the team. It is understood that the leader and members all give their opinions and come to consensus as to the best decision.

Before involving people at this level, the leader must consider:

- What risks am I taking? How important is this decision to the effectiveness of our operation? If the team wishes to take a route different from what I see as best and the decision proves not to be the best one, to what extent can it jeopardize our success?
- Am I able to present my ideas and listen to others with an open mind?
- Am I ready to support the decision of the team if it differs from my solution?
- Why am I asking the team to share the decision? Do team members have experience, knowledge, insights, and skills that will be valuable to the process and that I may lack? Is consensus essential for the group to support the decision?

If the leader is hesitant about his answer to any of these questions, he probably should involve the team at Level III, instead of Level II.

Level III Contributing to the Decision

At this level, people are asked to share information, ideas, or insights they hold on a particular topic. The input they provide will be considered, along with all other information the manager holds, in making the decision.

At all levels, clarifying exactly who is making the decision and how is important, but particularly at this level, as this is where unrealistic expectations most frequently arise. Often the manager asks, "What do you think about . . . " He does not clarify, "I have a decision to make. I'd like your opinion so that I will have all information available to use in making that decision." Too often meetings end with members of a group assuming the decision will go their way.

The other key to success at this level is to get back to people who have taken time to give their ideas. Let them know what decision was made and to whatever extent possible, why it was made.

Level IV Discussion of an Imposed Decision

The emphasis here is, "How can we make it work?" or if the decision is viewed negatively, "How can we best cope with it?" This is the most basic level of participation. Employees are not invited to offer opinions on the decision either because it is imposed from outside their immediate sphere of authority or because the individuals affected do not have the knowledge or experience to contribute to this particular decision. This level is used most frequently when an unpopular change is being introduced. It can be important in lessening or preventing resistance.

All levels of participation require strong group facilitation skills. This level, however, requires facilitating skills sufficiently well honed to prevent discussion from degenerating into a "bitch" session. The decision is a "fact of life" and is not open for review. The objective is to allow staff to voice fears and concerns, to come to terms with this "fact of life," and to take responsibility for coping with their concerns and ultimately assimilating the change.

This, then, is the bottom level of participation because staff do not contribute to the decision itself. It is much more process than task oriented, and yet it may be essential in minimizing resistance to change and supporting a positive climate.

If participation is to be productive, participants must understand at what level they are functioning and must be involved at the right level.

Who to Involve When: The Criteria

In deciding who to involve at what level, the following questions should be considered:

- Who will be affected by the decision?
- Do those directly affected have the skills, knowledge, and experience to contribute productively to the decision-making process?

- Who has valuable information and experience to bring to the decision-making process?
- Who has the appropriate technical as well as group decision-making skills?
- What is our time frame for making the decision?
- Who has the authority to make the final decision?

These facts interplay differently in different circumstances.

A woman attending a workshop on Participation and Teamwork announced first thing in the morning that "This stuff doesn't work." It was evident she wasn't attending the session of her own volition. When asked what experiences had suggested to her that it didn't work, she explained that she was on faculty at a college and that her dean believed in participation. In the interest of participation, he had decided that the faculty should rewrite the curriculum. Most of them had not done curriculum development before and were very busy people. It took them over a year of using every extra minute they could find including lunch breaks, and the results were mediocre. It was a foolish waste of time, she felt, and a consultant should have been hired to write the curriculum.

Quite likely a consultant should have been hired. The dean had involved his faculty at Level I and had asked them not only to make all decisions, but also to execute the project. The time available and their experience would suggest that Level II or III would have been appropriate. The consultant would have developed the curriculum considering their advice (Level III) and depending upon their skills in curriculum evaluation, they possibly could have shared the approval of the final product with the dean (Level II).

The variables are many, but basically when people have experience or information to contribute to a decision or when a decision which affects them is an important one, they need to be involved at some level.

Management Motive

Another participation pitfall can be management's understanding or use of participation. Some managers see participation primarily as a motivational tool. Consequently, employees may be given opportunities for involvement but in projects or issues that are peripheral to the operation or to their jobs. The following comment describes the frustration that results: "Oh, we have the opportunity to be involved all right, but always in projects that are on the periphery of the organization — things that don't really matter to the business we're in, like the smoking policy or the seventy-fifth anniversary. They are things that are important in a way, but don't really make a difference to the organization's bottom line or to my doing my job more effectively."

The other more common situation that evolves from management using participation as a motivational tool only is token participation. Staff comment: "They ask us for our input but we never see any results." Most of us have at one time or another experienced being asked for our opinion when we knew darn well that the decision had already been made. When employees sense their ideas are not being used, they soon quit contributing.

A service organization, committed to moving its culture toward increased participation, consistently asked employees for their opinions. At first, staff was committed to and excited about the new way of doing things. But when employees invested energy in participation and saw few results, the enthusiasm soon waned. "They're [management] not walking what they are talking," they complained. "They ask us for our input, but we never see any results." Employees decided to quit participating. A questionnaire that was subsequently sent out to collect information on their experiences with a particular customer-service program received less than a ten percent response.

In instances where participation most completely fulfills its potential of enriching organizations and their employees, managers recognize that it is the productive outcome of participation and the resulting sense of contribution and accomplishment that motivate, not the participation process alone. When participation works, the management motive is clear. We involve people because we believe that participation will produce better decisions and will increase the effectiveness of their implementation.

Limp Belief:

Participation → ↑ Motivation

Flexible Leadership Belief:

Productive Participation → Better Results → ↑ Motivation

3

Meeting with Success

Controlling Meeting Madness

Essential to Productive Participation are group skills. We have become more acutely aware of the need for effective group skills as the number of meetings in our organizations has dramatically increased. We are meeting more and too often enjoying it less. Meetings frequently are neither efficient nor effective. Yet meetings are essential to teamwork, participation, and generally for organizational effectiveness.

I often ask seminar participants how many of them are attending fewer meetings than two or three years ago. I seldom see any hands. One day two hands went up. It turned out that these individuals were both from the same organization. When I asked why they were attending fewer meetings, I was delighted to hear that their organization had recognized that many meetings weren't productive and had reassessed the purpose of each. The result was that several were disbanded. This organization had paused and examined its meetings. This objective look at why we bring a group together, how we work when we do come together, and what we achieve is not happening often enough.

Many organizations do not need to meet less. Indeed, many need to meet more, but most need to meet better. When the announcement of a meeting produces groans, sighs of resignation, and a "not another meeting!" response, it is a definite sign that meetings aren't productive.

Some meeting organizers have come to accept these signs as normal. "People," they say, "don't necessarily like meetings, but they're going to have to adapt because that's the way of the new organizational world." However, in most cases the issue is not that people are resisting something new, but that people are resisting something nonproductive. Productive meetings produce a "That was a great meeting!" response from the participants. You don't have to coax, cajole, and order those people to the next meeting.

When an organization has a limited training budget, is emphasizing teams, task forces, and committees, and asks where it should put its money, I most often suggest investing in the development of facilitation and meeting skills. When I suggest that the organization cost its meeting time and estimate how much of that time is wasted, I don't have to "sell" it any further on the need to increase its effectiveness in this area.

Try this for yourself:

- Think of a meeting you attend regularly.
- Calculate, based on your salary, the cost of your attendance.
- Calculate the approximate cost of each of the other members in attendance.
- Total the cost and multiply it by the number of meetings per month or year.

Now consider the number of different meetings taking place in your organization. If an organization of 400 people, with an average salary of $30,000 per year, had weekly departmental meetings of one hour for everyone, those meetings alone would cost the organization approximately $6,000 per week.

Some very simple steps can greatly increase the return on meeting investment time. Essential to productive meetings are:

- facilitation skills;
- a definition of purpose;
- preparation;
- meeting management know-how.

Balancing Task and Process:
The Art of the Facilitator

At one time it was believed that management didn't require any particular skill. It was assumed that once one was given the title of manager and whatever authority went with it, the rest would come naturally. Fortunately, most organizations now recognize that superior management and leadership depend upon well-developed skills.

Many organizations today view the meeting leader's role in much the way they once saw the role of the manager. If an individual is given the title of chairperson, a meeting room, and a flipchart, he should be able to do the job. The ineffective meetings that result are costly in terms of dollars as well as members' frustration. The successful balancing of task and process is particularly important to the meeting facilitator's performance.

He must ensure that everyone participates, that differing points of view are sufficiently explored, and when appropriate, that consensus is reached in order to accomplish the prescribed end within the allotted time.

In the rigid organization, when an upcoming meeting is the topic of discussion, one often hears, "Who's going to run the meeting?" In a rigid work group, that is just what the meeting leader does: he runs it. In this scenario, the chairperson sees his prime responsibility as that of control. The responsibility of the chairperson or departmental manager leading the meeting is usually seen to include setting the agenda and "getting through" as many items as possible within the allotted time. The emphasis is on "getting through" rather than the effectiveness of the process and the usefulness of the results.

The limp meeting leader emphasizes process over task believing it is more important that everything be aired and that everyone be heard than the desired results be accomplished or the time frame worked within. Although this may occasionally be appropriate when a sensitive issue is being discussed, if process is consistently given priority over the meeting of objectives, little will be accomplished.

The flexible meeting leader quickly recognizes when a discussion has gone beyond the point of being useful. On the other hand, he knows when a decision is being made too quickly without sufficient evaluation. He is attuned to hidden agendas and feelings and accurately senses when it is important to probe and bring them to the surface and when it is best to ignore them. He knows when it is necessary to pause to resolve conflict and when it is necessary to get on with the task at hand. In short, he skilfully balances task and process.

Most of us have experienced meetings that didn't work. In fact, some of them were probably disasters. They were stressful to sit through, and we considered it a great blessing that we weren't chairing the meeting. These meetings were seen as out of control, or a waste of time, or both.

Defining the Purpose

Reaching the desired outcome seems almost impossible when meeting members do not want to cooperate. Nonproductive behavior such as negativity, tuning out, monopolizing, and heated conflict over issues are a bane to most facilitators. The facilitator does well in this situation to make it through the agenda. She can become preoccupied with crowd control and have little opportunity to gather information to produce meeting results. These nonproductive behaviors and group interactions are often the result of poor planning. In particular, they are often the result of not having clearly defined the purpose of the meeting.

You have probably experienced being asked to attend a meeting whose purpose you were unsure of. You may have been given the topic: "We're going to have a meeting on the new management information system." That didn't give you any idea of the purpose. The purpose could have been to give you information, to get your opinion, or to sell you on the system. If you believed you were there to give your opinion and the individual calling the meeting had already made a decision and wanted to sell you on his choice, it is unlikely that the purpose either one of you had in mind would have been achieved. Common meeting purposes include:

- sharing decision-making;
- problem identification;
- information sharing;
- brainstorming for ideas;
- sharing a task;
- selling an idea;
- motivating;
- developing relationships.

A meeting may have multiple purposes, but the primary purpose should be identified by the individual calling the meeting and made clear to everyone invited. Three primary meeting purposes are decision-making, discussion (including providing input), and information. Generally, the fewer the purposes, the more effective the meeting.

The other aspect of purpose that needs to be considered is the function of a particular group. For example, a group's mandate may be to develop an orientation program for new employees. It is important to keep both the group's larger purpose, developing an orientation program, and the specific meeting purpose or task, perhaps brainstorming for ideas, in focus.

Mixed or unrealistic expectations are an obvious result of lack of definition of purpose. There are many additional ramifications that can sabotage a meeting's effectiveness. Lack of definition may mean:

- insufficient opportunity to assess whether a meeting is the best vehicle for fulfilling the purpose;
- the appropriate members may not be invited;
- inappropriate members may be invited;
- agenda items may not be appropriate;
- meeting members cannot come prepared.

Ultimately, it is unlikely that productive results will be achieved.

Is a Meeting the Best Vehicle?

Once the purpose of a meeting has been defined and assessed, we may decide that a meeting is not the best method of accomplishing the purpose. We do not frequently enough hear teams ask, "What do we want to accomplish in this meeting?" and "Is a meeting the best way to accomplish it?" If the purpose is to share information or to update people, we should consider whether a meeting is the most efficient method of communication.

Some information does need to be shared personally either one-on-one or in a meeting. Generally, this is information that requires personal contact and discussion. It could include:

- selling an idea;
- presenting complex information that requires detailed explanation, questions, and answers; and
- information concerning a change that may be resisted.

Ensuring the Appropriate People Are Invited

When people doze in meetings or mentally write their grocery lists, they either should not be present or don't understand why they are present and the role they are meant to play. People don't tune out when the issue is of importance to them and they understand how they can contribute.

Too often the wrong people are invited to a meeting. If the definition of the purpose of the meeting is kept in mind when developing the list of participants, this can be prevented. The main considerations in developing the meeting invitation list are: Who have the skills, experience, or knowledge that are needed if we are to fulfill our purpose? And, who are directly involved in or affected by the topic under discussion? The meeting leader who not only communicates the purpose, but lets people know how they can contribute and that their participation is valued, seldom has to endure meeting attendees who are present in body only.

Less common but equally important is the situation in which appropriate people are not involved in a meeting. In this case, the desired results cannot be met because the individuals who hold needed information, experience, or authority are not present. In this situation, the time participants invest in attending the meeting is wasted.

Another aspect of group makeup which should be determined according to the meeting's purpose is group size. If the meeting, for example, is for discussion and decision-making purposes, more than nine people can be counterproductive.

Ensuring Appropriate Agenda Topics

Groups that meet regularly are often not sufficiently vigilant about the items that are discussed during their valuable time. I once sat in on a management meeting that covered such disparate topics as the introduction of a new product, a marketing budget, the rearrangement of parking spaces in the parking lot, and whether or not the receptionist should be drinking coffee at her desk. The two latter topics sparked much more heated discussion and, therefore, took much more time than the first two items. The topics which took most of the group's time did not contribute to the purpose of the management group which was to direct product development and marketing.

A group that meets regularly needs to define the specific purpose of its meeting. Once the definition has been agreed upon, that definition then should be used as a measurement tool to determine whether or not agenda items are appropriate. The facilitator should also keep the purpose clearly in mind in monitoring the ad hoc discussion topics which arise informally during the meeting. Because a particular topic sparks interest in a group does not necessarily mean that it is appropriate or productive for the group to discuss. Too often topics discussed fall within the realm of someone else's authority, pertain to only a few of the members, or are not sufficiently important to warrant the time of the entire group.

Ensuring Prepared and Focused Meeting Partners

A final application of the definition of meeting purpose is ensuring prepared and focused meeting members.

When meeting members talk at cross-purposes and have very different ideas of where the discussion should be going, they often have different interpretations of the purpose of the meeting. If a purpose is not defined, each individual assumes one and develops meeting expectations according to that perceived purpose. The result can be a room full of very different and often opposing and unrealistic expectations. This leads to disagreement, conflict, and if a decision is required, a long and circuitous route to that end.

Meetings are most productive when participants come prepared. If they do not have information pertaining to the purpose, little valid preparation can take place. Coming prepared may include members up-dating themselves on information on a particular issue; gathering pertinent material to bring to the meeting; or perhaps most importantly developing their own thoughts on a particular issue. When members come unprepared, a great deal of time is wasted while they get into gear, obtain basic information, or work through misperceptions. Meetings to which individuals come prepared with a clear sense of purpose move immediately into a productive mode.

The definition of purpose has many applications. Most importantly, it can ensure that the right people are in attendance, that they are able to come prepared, and that they understand how they can contribute. If these applications are used, it is unlikely that the facilitator will be faced with an impossible task.

Meeting Management Know-How

Developing the Agenda
It is interesting to watch how agendas are or are not used in organizations. The arrival of an agenda on a desk may command little notice. The more regular a meeting, the less attention its agenda appears to attract. It is often merely glanced at as the recipient sorts through his or her "in" basket.

An agenda is frequently viewed as a mere notice or reminder

of a meeting. If this is the perceived purpose, then of course the participant only needs to check the top couple of lines to ascertain which meeting and when. The rest of the agenda is often treated as a for-your-information-only item and is or is not scanned depending upon the recipient's interest and the time available. The agenda is then quickly filed or put into a holding tray to be retrieved just before dashing off to the meeting.

Only "passive" agendas that are merely meeting to-do lists can be treated in this way. An "active" agenda that provides useful information is difficult to ignore. It serves several purposes before and during the meeting. Prior to the meeting, the facilitator uses it as a planning tool and participants as a preparatory tool. During the meeting, the facilitator and participants use the agenda as a guide and time-management tool.

A Planning Tool

An agenda is not only a planning tool but its development is ideally a planning process. Before any item is accepted as an agenda item, it must be tested against the purpose of the meeting to determine its legitimacy, as discussed earlier. This ensures that each agenda item is carrying the group toward the fulfillment of that purpose.

In planning the order of a meeting, the priority of each item must be considered. When possible, the most important and controversial items should not be first, as a group requires warm-up time. Neither should they come at the end, when members are running out of energy and may be anxious to leave.

Developing an agenda forces a facilitator to deal with the issue of time and to make some pre-meeting decisions about what realistically can and cannot be accomplished.

Those who develop the agenda, control the meeting. If teamwork is to take place, it is important that all participants contribute in some way to the agenda. In fit teams, all members have the opportunity to contribute to agenda items. The role of the facilitator often rotates, allowing different members the opportunity to develop an agenda.* The team, however, establishes the criteria for selecting and prioritizing agenda items. The individual whose turn it is to take the role of facilitator uses these criteria in developing the agenda.

A Preparatory Tool

A list of topics to be covered does not provide meeting members with sufficient information. If an agenda is to be used as a catalyst for preparation, an objective is required for each item. One method of effectively providing the required information and also reinforcing the expectation that everyone comes prepared is to add a heading "Please come prepared to . . . "

The agenda can also act as a guide and time-management tool. A common dilemma faced by facilitators is that sufficient meeting time never seems available. In reality, the problem is not the lack of time, but the fact that the meeting time at our disposal is often not well managed. Allotting time per agenda item has become a common practice. When this is done, the agenda becomes a simple time-management tool. If followed, it assists the facilitator in keeping the meeting on time. If an item appears to require more discussion time than allotted, the timed agenda forces the group to make an immediate decision about how to handle the limited time remaining. The facilitator leads the group in a quick assessment of whether this particular topic is of sufficient immediate importance to continue the discussion, and if so, which item or items can be postponed until another meeting.

Active agendas breathe life into a meeting. If an agenda is to be active, it requires thoughtful development, includes sufficient information, and is used by all meeting members.

---

* The facilitator's role should rotate only to individuals who have the skills to fulfill the role effectively. Some groups see rotating the facilitator's role as an opportunity to increase ownership and participation. If everyone does not have the appropriate skills and confidence, however, the meetings are unsuccessful and participation is ultimately hurt rather than helped.

Facilitator's Personal Preparation

The facilitator who prepares himself well for a meeting is truly able to conduct it. The experienced symphony conductor who is not familiar with a score might make it through a performance, but the quality of the performance would be questionable. Similarly, the meeting facilitator who is not well prepared cannot hope to orchestrate a meeting effectively. Only with preparation will he recognize when enough time has been spent on a particular aspect of a topic, when another aspect has not been sufficiently explored, and which meeting members to call upon to clarify or provide an expert opinion. This does not mean that the facilitator needs to be an expert on every agenda topic, but the most effective meeting facilitators ensure that they are sufficiently well briefed to be able to orchestrate the discussion and bring it effectively to closure.

Clarifying Objectives

A few moments at the beginning of a meeting to clarify objectives is time well spent, even if objectives have been previously described in agendas or meeting notices. Advanced information may not have been read or may have been misinterpreted. Five minutes to ensure that everyone is on the same track can save the entire meeting.

In addition, it gives everyone the opportunity to "get into" the meeting. In most organizations today, people are literally running to meetings, often leaving tasks unfinished and certainly leaving part of their minds back with their previous tasks. Clarifying objectives, like the silent generation of ideas, can give members time to clear their minds of what was going on a few moments before and become involved in the moment.

Final Recap of the Commitments to Action

In Chapter 1, I referred to an employee-involvement committee meeting in which consensus had been mistakenly assumed. The following dialogue takes you to the group's next meeting in which they discovered what had happened and explored why.

The facilitator, Susan Barnes, opened the meeting.

SUSAN: "I want to update you on activities since our last meeting. We sent out a memo this morning to let people know that the minutes of our meetings are available to anyone, and we posted last week's minutes in the library."

DON: "What? I thought we had decided not to post the minutes."

KATHY: "Yes! That's what I thought, too."

MARK: "Me, too. We sure talked long enough about it, and I left here thinking we had decided that opening our minutes to people might raise unrealistic expectations or cause misconceptions by giving only part information."

DAVE: "No way. Most of us were strongly for posting them."

A heated discussion began on what the decision had actually been. Susan intervened.

SUSAN: "I feel a little silly. I'm not sure what happened, but I do remember saying, 'It looks like we have consensus,' and no one disagreed."

MARK: "Yes, but you didn't say consensus on what, and I guess we each filled in the blank with our own point of view."

SUSAN· "I believe those of you opposing sat back and didn't have much to say toward the end of the discussion, and I guess I erroneously assumed that you had been won over."

FRANK: "You know something else? We ran late last week and dashed off after the last agenda item. We didn't do any kind of wrap-up."

SUSAN: "You're right. If I'd made sure we had time for a recap of our decisions and commitments to action, we would have caught it. It looks like I need to be more careful in checking for consensus. Please remind me if I'm ever not specific enough, and I have to make sure we have time for a recap at the end of every meeting."

The elements of a meeting that can be most critical to its

success are for the most part simple. Recapping a meeting does not require any particular skill and takes little time. It must, however, be scheduled and seen as a priority or — as in the above example — it won't happen.

A recap serves many purposes. Most obviously it confirms what has been decided upon. The facilitator establishes consensus, checks for understanding, and ensures that specific commitments to action are assigned to each item and that individuals understand their roles in implementing the decisions.

The recap for the meeting of the employee-involvement group might have included: "We have decided that the minutes for our meetings will be made available to everyone. Frank will send out a memo on Monday letting employees know that the minutes are available. Sheila will post a copy of today's minutes in the library on Monday and will take the responsibility for posting them each week."

A recap leaves no room for misunderstandings. It also increases the likelihood that individuals will follow through on their personal commitments.

Another important benefit of recapping is the creation of a sense of accomplishment. Once the facilitator has completed a recap, the reaction is often, "Wow, we accomplished a lot." People leave the meeting energized and looking forward to the next meeting when they know their time has been well spent.

Recapping can have an additional benefit for task forces and committees. For these groups, developing and maintaining a positive image within the organization is usually very important. Committees and task forces are watched by all sorts of people: the managers to whom the group reports; the managers and supervisors to whom committee members report, who may have to run their unit short staffed when the member is involved in committee work; and co-workers who are often carrying an extra load while the member is in meetings. These people, of course, are watching for results. Is the time taken and the extra work required worth the gains? They often have as much investment in the time spent in the committee meetings as do the actual participants. A critical success factor for most committees, then, is that they be seen as productive by the rest of the organization.

Recapping assists each member in playing an important public-relations role. Meeting members are often queried about meetings. If they are not able to convey an image of productivity, the committee can have an uphill battle. When the response to "What happened at the meeting today?" is "Well, let's see. We talked about the minutes, whether they should be available to everyone and had a lot of discussion on that one, and . . . " the listener is unlikely to be impressed.

When the meeting has been recapped, however, meeting members leave with a concise list of accomplishments that is in the forefront of their minds, at easy reach. A committee member is much more impressive when she can quickly respond to queries of co-workers with energy and specifics: "We decided a, b, c, et cetera."

Defining the purpose of a meeting, planning it well, clarifying its objectives, and recapping the commitments to action do not exempt the leader from any responsibility for developing and demonstrating facilitating skills. However, planning and organization do make the task much simpler. If the organizational and management elements are in place, the leader is freed to facilitate. He can concentrate on the delicate balancing of task and process, conducting the meeting members' comments, pulling out more information here, highlighting there, and closing somewhere else to create the results that fulfill the meeting's objectives. Although well-honed facilitating skills are always a benefit, proper preparation and structure can create meetings which flow with ease toward their objectives and make the novice meeting leader look like a pro.

4

Reaching Consensus

Getting Beyond "Can Everybody Live With It?"

We emphasize that the best teams consist of individuals who do not think alike. Skilled facilitators encourage the expression of differing points of view, they create an environment of honesty and openness, they establish the expectation that everyone is responsible for contributing ideas, and so substantially increase the volume of ideas and, therefore, options created by the team. Facilitators who do all of the above well create another challenge for themselves: How to bring the many different and perhaps opposing points of view together to reach consensus?

In the previous chapter, we followed a meeting of an employee-involvement group. The following excerpt from another meeting of the same group is a prime example of the difficulty a facilitator can face in trying to get a group to come to consensus. Although the example we are using is that of a committee, the dilemma faced by the facilitator is common in all types of teams.

The employee-involvement committee's mandate was to lower the decision-making within the organization. The committee's first task was to identify opportunities for employee involvement. Members soon had a list of forty-five suggestions. Because they were limited by the number of members on the committee as well as by time and experience, they decided they could not handle several projects at once and, therefore, had to choose one with which to begin.

The committee fairly easily narrowed the forty-five sugges-tions down to three. Of the forty-five, it decided the most appropriate and important issues were: the lack of photocopying facilities; the smoking policy; the car policy. It had been fairly easy to reach this point, and Susan Barnes, the chairperson, was confident that the members could easily complete their task at their two-hour Monday meeting. At the meeting, Susan suggested that as the first step in their decision-making pro-cess the committee members discuss each of the three options.

The first option put forward was the car policy. Most com-mittee members showed little enthusiasm, but two committee members, who happened to be in the sales division and drove company cars, were adamant that this was the most impor-tant item on the list. The car policy hadn't been updated for three years they said. It was a long-outstanding issue and one they believed employees should have an opportunity to be involved in. This was definitely the most important issue, and they were, they indicated, firm in their choice.

The smoking policy received more general support as many people were unhappy with the present policy. Not everyone, however, was willing to accept it as the most important issue to be addressed, and one committee member, a smoker, who believed any policy violated smokers' rights, was adamant that this was not an appropriate issue for the employee-involvement group.

The group was now three-quarters of an hour into the meet-ing, and it had not begun to make progress. Susan, however, held hope for the last option, the photocopying facilities. This seemed to be a less contentious issue, and she expected the group could reach agreement on this one.

Susan's optimism did not last as strong pros and cons emerged. Two individuals who walked up a flight of stairs and stood in line several times a day in order to use a photocopier supported the issue and couldn't see how either of the other two issues came close to this one in importance. Susan began feeling a little panicky. Members had spent over half of their time discussing the options, and rather than bringing them toward consensus, the discussions seemed to have pulled them farther apart. How was she going to get the group to reach a decision in fifty minutes? Fortunately, Susan realized that the most immediate issue was not what their decision should be, but how they were going to reach a decision.

The most common cause of sluggish group decision-making is the lack of a decision-making game plan and agreed-upon rules. The committee hadn't established how it would make its decision. Were members going to vote and accept a majority rule? Were they going to reach consensus? If so, what steps would they take in order to reach a decision? When these predecisions are made, decision-making on the issue at hand is greatly simplified.

Majority rule is the simplest method of decision-making. It is clean-cut and takes less time than reaching consensus. The majority method, however, has two limitations:

- The majority is not always right; and
- The minority who did not "win" can sabotage the decision if it has been an either/or or win/lose situation.

No decision, however made, of course is guaranteed to be "right." Nevertheless, when a majority method is used, the reasons for opposing a chosen action and the alternatives are often not sufficiently explored.

A frequent complaint about group decision-making is that it takes too long. My experience is that too often groups don't take long enough, particularly if majority rule is their chosen method. (Often the majority method is not chosen; it is simply the most obvious method and no one has considered an alternative.)

A case in point was an automated-systems task force which needed to collect information from the users. The task force had already decided that personal interviews were required and that the information was not of a confidential nature. The decision that needed to be made was whether the interviewer should conduct the interview at the user's work station or whether the user should be interviewed in an interviewing room.

Discussion was brief. One member suggested that supervisors might be upset if employees were asked to leave their posts for interviews. Meeting members agreed and cited the additional concern that work time would be wasted as the employee traveled to and from the interviewing room.

"Is everyone in agreement, then, that we should interview at the work station?" asked the chairperson.

Everyone nodded.

One member questioned, "Do you think we've looked at this carefully enough?"

Another quickly reacted, "Come on, Dick. We all agreed. Let's count our blessings and get on with the next item. We've got a lot to cover."

Other members murmured in agreement. A committee member was chosen to draw up an interviewing schedule, and the group moved quickly on to the next topic. The committee covered a long list of agenda items in one hour, and everyone left feeling that the group had had a very efficient and productive meeting.

When the interviews were conducted, however, various problems arose. Although the questions were not of a confidential nature, some questions did ask for an opinion and some individuals felt uncomfortable about giving their opinions in an open-concept office. They feared that their opinion might differ from that of their supervisor. Many interruptions occurred, and as a result, some interviews took much longer than planned. Supervisors found the interviews interruptive to their work units and complained to senior management, who then questioned the committee's management of the project.

Why were such obvious possible drawbacks not considered?

- the group came to agreement quickly;
- none of the committee members had any particular personal interest in the topic;

- no one played devil's advocate or challenged the group to examine the possible negatives.

When time is a scarce commodity and everyone has experienced the frustration of difficult decision-making sessions, people generally take pride and pleasure in quick decisions. When easy consensus is reached, meeting members who suggest that an issue should be further discussed are taking a risk because their position is usually quickly put down.

Meeting members and facilitators in particular need to be on guard against too-quick decisions. In this case, the chairperson might have said, "Let's take a minute to make sure we haven't overlooked anything. Does interviewing at the work station pose any potential problems which we should consider?" Again, the facilitator must find a very fine balance. In this example, it is between effectiveness and efficiency.

The Power of the Minority

When majority rule is the chosen decision-making method, the result can be winners and losers. The minority group that doesn't agree with the decision can intentionally or unintentionally have a negative impact on the outcome. If these members leave the meeting with no interest in making the decision work, their lack of active support can be detrimental. If their apathy toward the decision spreads to others in the organization, the negative effect can be considerable. The negative force created can be even more powerful, however, if the minority members leave the meeting vocally discontented. This case most often occurs when a minority believes its point of view was not fairly heard or that a decision was pushed through by a power group.

How decisions are made reflects the group's level of development. A fit team aims for consensus. Groups often consider that reaching a decision "everyone can live with" is about as close to consensus as they can get. In fact, many groups consider that if everyone can live with a decision, then they *have* reached consensus.

"Living with it" is an impassive phrase. It conveys no suggestion of energy, enthusiasm, or drive. In most cases, everyone leaves the meeting room half-happy; no one is particularly committed to making the decision work. It is frequently the result of a dangerous compromise.

Dangerous Compromise

Compromise is essential to any teamwork and team decision-making, but compromise can be dangerous when a team is determined to reach a decision that "everyone can live with." Too often good decisions are compromised. In an effort to please everyone, excellent ideas become diluted to the point of mediocrity. This is not the intent in striving for consensus. True consensus is a driving force that turns decisions into actions.

Consensus is often not chosen as the decision-making method because it is seen as too time consuming a method and too idealistic a goal. Consensus suggests that everyone should agree. To ask that everyone agree that a decision is the best possible choice is perhaps idealistic even for a fit team, particularly when teams are frequently cross-functional or multidisciplinary groups.

The task of reaching consensus becomes much less onerous when a group takes three steps before entering the actual decision-making process. It should:

- come to an agreement on a definition of consensus;
- develop a back-up plan as to how members will make a decision if the team cannot reach consensus;
- identify a method for reaching consensus.

The Definition of Consensus

The aim of most teams is not that everyone be in full agreement with a decision. What is strived for is agreement to support the decision. The definition of consensus used by most teams is *agreement to support the decision 100 percent.*

This definition requires that disagreement does not go outside the meeting room. Once a decision has been made, it becomes "our decision" and each member agrees to present it as such and to do everything within his power to make it work. In some groups, this commitment is almost as great a challenge as getting everyone to agree that a particular decision is "the best." However, developing a method for reaching consensus greatly facilitates the process. The ease with which this definition of consensus is fulfilled also depends upon the development level of the group. Teams that have spent time developing cohesiveness generally find that reaching consensus is not a very difficult task.

The Back-Up Plan

The back-up plan determines before the decision-making process begins how the team will make a decision should members not be able to reach their definition of consensus. The back-up plan might be to have the leader make the decision, taking into consideration the ideas which have been presented by the team, to have a resident expert on a particular topic make the decision, or to accept a majority rule.

Steps to Reaching Consensus

Describing the Best Decision

A most important step in reaching consensus is describing at the outset of the decision-making process what the best decision looks like from the point of view of the team. When this has not been defined, each individual team member has a picture of the best decision, which he or she is working toward. The result is often team members pulling in many different directions toward many different "best" solutions.

The example of the employee-involvement committee that was cited earlier demonstrates this. The salespeople, smokers, nonsmokers, and individuals responsible for photocopying each had different personal priorities in mind and very different ideas of what constituted the "best" decision. Only when they asked, "What is the best decision from the point of view of this team?" were they able to move forward. The best decision from a team perspective had nothing to do with whether one did or did not drive a company car or whether one smoked. The best decision was one which led the team toward fulfilling its mandate. Its mandate was to lower decision-making in the organization.

The committee described the best decision as one that:

- lowered decision-making in the organization;
- did not take a great deal of time (the members had only a few hours per week to devote to committee work);
- did not require a large budget (as the committee was new and had not had an opportunity to develop credibility with senior management, it decided it should begin conservatively);
- affected the most people (after all, this was an employee-involvement group);
- contributed most directly to the organization's bottom line (a major purpose of increased employee involvement, members reasoned);
- the group had the skills to execute.

What resulted was a list of decision-making criteria. It was quite simple to assess which option met more criteria. Most importantly, this description of the best decision moved individuals from a subjective perspective to an objective team view.

Options	Criteria					
	Lowers decision-making	Affects the most people	Is not time intensive	Does not require a large budget	Benefits the organization's bottom line	We have the required skills
Car Policy	✔		✔	✔		✔
Smoking Policy	✔	✔	✔	✔		✔
Photo-copying Facilities	✔	✔	✔	✔	✔	✔

Note: In this case, the option which fit most criteria fell out easily. In some cases, it is useful to weight the criteria. The criteria most heavily weighted become the priority items.

Establishing decision-making criteria is a common decision-making technique used by individuals, and yet somehow when several people get together to make a decision, it is often overlooked.

Exploring the Minority Position

Reaching the team definition of consensus — willingness to support a decision 100 percent — is made easier when a group ensures that the minority position is sufficiently explored. Individuals are more easily able to support a decision with which they don't agree 100 percent if their point of view has been thoughtfully considered in the decision-making process.

An additional benefit of exploring the minority position is the possible discovery that a minority idea may be an important one. Minority ideas are often the more creative. Generally, in groups it is the minority who thinks laterally and the majority who thinks vertically. Edward de Bono, who coined the phrase "lateral thinking," described vertical thinking as digging the same hole deeper and lateral thinking as digging a new hole somewhere else. The most effective decisions result from groups pausing to explore holes that team members are trying to dig somewhere else.

Team Workouts for Developing Productive Participation

Workout: To increase meeting effectiveness.

Background: This workout highlights the fact that everyone, not only the facilitator, is responsible for the effectiveness of meetings.

Steps:

1. At the end of a meeting have members respond to and discuss the following questions. Ensure that you set aside sufficient time. The time you require will depend upon the group's level of development.

   Preparation
   (i)   Did everyone understand the purpose of the meeting?
   (ii) Did everyone have the agenda in sufficient time to prepare?
   (iii) Did everyone prepare?
   (iv) In the meeting, were members able to fulfill any commitments they had made for the meeting (e.g. bring information, make reports, et cetera)?
   (v)   Do members know how to get an item on the agenda?

   Process and discussion
   (i)   Were the objectives in discussing each item made clear?
   (ii) Did we stay on track?

(iii) Did we all participate?

(iv) Did we listen to each other's ideas?

(v) Were we receptive to others' ideas?

(vi) Were we willing to change our position if a reasonable argument was presented?

(vii) Did we probe for clarification if positions or ideas were unclear?

(viii) Did we recap periodically?

(ix) Were we comfortable being honest and open?

(x) Did we have a final recap of commitments to action for each item including who is responsible and when?

Decision-making

(i) Was a decision/commitment to action made for each agenda item?

(ii) Was everyone comfortable with the outcome of each decision?

(iii) Does everyone feel his or her point of view was heard and considered?

(iv) Does everyone know what each decision is?

(v) Do we know who is responsible for putting each decision into action?

(vi) Is a follow-up system in place to ensure decisions become actions?

2. Highlight any items that did not receive a strong yes.

3. Using the highlighted items, discuss appropriate commitments to action for increased meeting effectiveness.

Workout: To identify the causes of nonproductive participation and to make commitments to action for making participation more productive or to audit the team's participation process.

Steps: **1.** Have each team member complete the following assessment.

Participation Assessment

The following statements are designed to assess the effectiveness of our participation process. Please rate the extent to which each statement describes our team.

   1 not at all
   2 somewhat
   3 to a great extent
   4 definitely

If you rate a statement a 1 or a 2, please give an example under Evidence.

When asked to participate, we know how
our input will be used.   **1**   **2**   **3**   **4**

Evidence (if 1 or 2):

_____

_____

_____

We implement most decisions without
reworking them.   **1**   **2**   **3**   **4**

Evidence (if 1 or 2):

_____

_____

_____

When asked to participate, we know
to what extent our participation will
influence the outcome. **1 2 3 4**

Evidence (if 1 or 2):

_____

_____

_____

The decisions we have made as a team
have proven effective. **1 2 3 4**

Evidence (if 1 or 2):

_____

_____

_____

When we meet, our time is well
spent. **1 2 3 4**

Evidence (if 1 or 2):

_____

_____

_____

The purpose for our meeting is
clear. **1 2 3 4**

Evidence (if 1 or 2):

_____

_____

_____

We have skills in reaching
consensus.   **1   2   3   4**

Evidence (if 1 or 2):

_____

_____

_____

2. If the questionnaire has been completed anonymously, share the output from the assessments
with the group.

or

If the group is sufficiently developed, ask team
members to share their responses with the group.

3. From responses and discussion, identify opportunities for improvement which the team can
control or influence. Opportunities may have
been noted on the questionnaire under Evidence.

4. Make commitments to action.

Note: Depending on the number of areas requiring improvement and
the meeting time available, additional meetings may be
required to complete steps 3 and 4.

Workout: To increase the facilitator's effectiveness.

Application: The following checklist can be used as an audit for the more experienced facilitator or as a developmental tool for the less experienced. As a developmental tool, it can be used by an observer who is acting as coach for the facilitator or by the facilitator herself. The facilitator should check this list before meetings, at break, and after meetings.

Eventually, the facilitator's familiarity with the list will be such that she will have it in the back of her mind throughout meetings. Initially, it would be wise to make a special note of any particularly challenging points and to keep them handy as a reminder throughout the meeting.

Once comfortable with her role, the facilitator should make an effort to check the list periodically. It is very easy to slip back into old habits.

A Checklist for Effective Facilitation

1. Does the facilitator clearly establish objectives at the outset of the meeting?
2. Is everyone participating?
3. Are there any signs of hidden agendas or concerns that are not being discussed?
4. Do we establish criteria for decision-making to ensure our decision is based on logic and will fulfill the need?
5. In attempting to reach consensus, are minority positions explored?
6. Does the facilitator ensure that new ideas or minority positions are explored before being dropped?
7. When everyone quickly comes to consensus, are efforts made to ensure that the topic is sufficiently explored

before the decision is reached? (i.e., Are the pros and cons sufficiently discussed?)

8. Does the facilitator check for consensus before decisions are made?
9. Does the facilitator guard against compromises that are really second-rate solutions?
10. Is the discussion productively on track?
11. Does the facilitator pull the discussion back on track when necessary?
12. Does the facilitator keep to the allotted time for agenda items?
13. Does the facilitator recap periodically?
14. Does the facilitator ensure that there is a decision for each agenda item requiring one?
15. Does the facilitator recap the decisions before closing?

Team Fitness Element 2
OPENNESS

5

The Challenge of Developing Openness

Openness, the perennial challenge to organizational effectiveness, requires even greater attention in an organization dedicated to teamwork. A group cannot function as a team without it. Openness is essential to critiquing, in whose absence little growth occurs. Openness is essential if the pros and cons of ideas are to be fully explored. Openness is essential if the best solution is to be chosen. Openness is essential if disagreements are to be worked through before they become disputes. Openness is essential if we are to capitalize on individual differences and so maximize teamwork.

Supplying organizations with the much-sought-after communication effectiveness workshops has been a lucrative business for many training firms over the past several years. Although many organizations have invested large sums to improve their employees' communication skills, the organizational need still most frequently identified is improved communication. Communication may include: resolving conflict, greater honesty and openness, and more sharing of ideas. Although employees may attend courses and develop their communication skills, they often do not effectively apply what they learn.

Openness occurs only in teams where members recognize the benefits of applying the skills that create openness and where members feel it is safe to be open. Trust, the ingredient essential to any good relationship, can be the most difficult to develop and the easiest to erode.

A Japanese executive responsible for a North American operation was asked his observations on building North American teams. He admitted that the task was a challenging one: "Everyone seems to ask the other fellow to trust him," he observed. "But no one seems to be willing to be the first to trust."

The trouble with trust is that it requires some level of risk taking. The team member wonders, what risk am I taking by:

- giving my honest opinion;
- sharing information;
- giving constructive criticism;
- admitting my errors;
- sharing my job responsibility;
- revealing a hidden agenda?

Trust develops most easily among individuals with a common experiential base. But today's work force is marked by diversity rather than commonality. It is made up of representatives of many different lifestyles and cultures, all bringing different and sometimes opposing values to bear on how the job should done. The result is a kaleidoscope of contrasting working and relating styles and methods.

In addition to learning to trust others whose personal experiences may differ greatly from our own, we must learn to trust individuals with organizational and professional experience which differs from our own. The proliferation of cross-functional and multidisciplinary teams means that more frequently individuals of very different professional backgrounds, with different views of the organization and different work values and priorities, are coming together as a team.

To succeed in this new world, we must learn to respond not from our preconceived idea of how a "systems guy" or a "human-resource person" or someone of a particular race does things, but we must start fresh and assess our personal experiences with some objectivity to begin to develop trust.

In being open, people sometimes perceive two types of risk: personal risk and career risk. Individuals who hesitate to be open because of personal risk usually fear that they will damage their personal image. They may fear that their ideas will be shot down in such a way that they will be wounded. They may fear that they will look foolish or not as bright as the rest. They may fear their comments could alienate their colleagues and even cause damage to their working relationships.

Those who remain closed for fear of risking retributions that could affect their career are usually responding to a damaging past experience. Some experiences are brought from previous patriarchal work groups where "father knows best," and compliance and agreement are rewarded with attention and, when possible, benefits and perks. People who are not compliant or who challenge ideas and methods are considered difficult and are counseled, and if that doesn't work, they are quietly moved off somewhere where they will be less of a nuisance. Although little openness exists in a paternalistic group, the signals as to what is accepted and what is not are quite clear.

A consultant who joined a new consulting firm was pleased to be invited on the first day of his new job to attend a senior partners' meeting. He felt that this invitation was definite proof that the organization was indeed an open and team-oriented one, as it had claimed in his interviews. During the meeting, the senior partner presented a new marketing plan. It so happened that the firm that my colleague had just left had recently implemented a similar marketing plan and so, when the senior partner asked for comments, he felt equipped to give useful information backed by experience. He talked about what had worked and what hadn't. When he was through, he was convinced that he had made his mark on the organization on his first day on the job.

Returning to his office, he walked down the hall with the partner to whom he reported. The partner looked at him and said, "What in the hell did you think you were doing in there?"

My friend, astounded, said, "What do you mean?"

The partner retorted, "When he asked for your input, do you think he expected an answer?"

Rigid authoritarian groups in which position is power create even greater threats to individuals who dare to be open. Team members who have experienced this kind of group often carry organizational battle scars that can take a good deal of time to heal. These individuals usually believe that they were victims. They believe that a poor performance rating or a lateral move, rather than a promotion, were the repercussions of their words or actions. Whether the relationship between the action and the result was real or perceived, the individuals believe that it was real. Since in the past repercussions were often slow in coming, the team member who has had damaging experiences in the past will not easily be convinced that things are different now. As one fellow who was beginning to open up commented, "No one jumps down my throat when I disagree, but how do I know they won't get me somehow later?"

Another issue which relates to perceived risk-taking at the career level is the extent to which individuals believe their organization is sincere about its commitment to teamwork. Staff often feel they receive mixed messages. On the one hand, they receive verbal confirmation that teamwork is important, but on the other hand, they frequently see stars rather than team players rewarded by promotions or choice projects. They then question how much they are risking by sharing openly with team members, particularly when being asked to share their expertise and their ideas. By sharing with other team members, they wonder if they may be making someone else a star and possibly jeopardizing their own opportunities. These individuals are usually willing to be honest and open in giving their opinions and constructive criticism. However, they are much more hesitant to share their expertise, ideas, and any "inside" information.

Many factors then contribute to the issue of trust:

- the individual's perception of self and his or her personal confidence;
- past experience which may include personal attacks or conflicts that did damage to the individual's career (real or perceived);
- differences brought to the team from different lifestyles, cultures, professions, or functions;

- disbelief that teamwork will be more greatly rewarded than star tactics.

All of these factors may be active in some teams. How, then, does one develop the trust required for openness when the challenge appears so great?

6

Creating an Environment of Openness

A participant in a workshop in which we were discussing the importance of the leader's role in team effectiveness rather angrily and adamantly commented, "It's not just the leader's responsibility!" She appeared frustrated by a sense that it was all up to her.

Indeed, in teamwork we work toward the opposite: the sharing of leadership and responsibility. However, before a group becomes a fit team, the responsibility for beginning and maintaining a team-fitness and development program is the leader's.

Certainly, when the work environment is not conducive to trust and openness, the leader must be the one to initiate change, by creating expectations of open behavior, by providing opportunities to develop a more open environment, and by personally and consistently displaying openness.

The Leader's Responsibility

At one time or another, most of us have worked with a leader who appeared to be open and who made others feel comfortable being open with him. Soon we may have become suspicious, however, that he was opening up just enough to convince us, while we were giving much more in return.

The one I remember best was a manager who had an honest, open look about him, wide eyes which always looked directly into yours, a ready smile, and open body gestures, such as open arms and open and up-turned palms. He talked a lot about being frank. "I'm a direct sort of guy," he would say. "I like to be open and honest with people." He would often start out statements with "To be honest" or "I thought it was important for you to know." It was easy to respond openly to this fellow. It didn't take long, however, to recognize that he was only open and honest about some things. It was what he left out that distorted the information. Basically, he was open when it served his purpose. His token openness produced no beneficial results. His group became a limp group, talking a lot but being careful not to disclose anything of real importance.

In the rigid organization information is hoarded and doled out very carefully and only to those most trusted. To be trusted, one must be in management, and so little important information reaches the people who most need it — those producing the product or dealing with the customer.

Management fears that information, though valuable, can be dangerous if it gets into the wrong hands and so information control is a priority. Information is shared on a need-to-know basis and the need must be critical before it happens. When deciding precisely what information should be shared, management asks, "What do we want them to know?" In contrast, in the flexible organization, the question is, "What do people need (and deserve) to know if they are to be a productive part of what is happening?"

In the flexible team, the leader sets the example of openness. Displaying openness requires the desire and willingness to share information. This does not mean that everyone should be told everything all of the time. It does mean that individuals should receive as much information as possible about the issues, decisions, and actions that will affect them. The leader who displays openness, demonstrates by example that he believes that this is the preferred way for the team to work. The leader committed to developing openness also challenges others to be open and takes responsibility for creating a risk-free environment.

Challenging Team Members to Be Open

In rigid or limp groups, signs of concern, disagreement, or discomfort are usually ignored in the hope that they will go away and that the person sending them will conform. The sentiment on the part of the leader is usually, "Why create problems by getting into something we don't have to?"

Closed members send signs of concern or disagreement via body language, unusual silence, and negative comments about particular issues to others but not to the leader. Since they are sending signs, they probably want to be open but don't know how or are not sure that it's acceptable. The leader of a fit team quickly checks out signs of closed resistance or disagreement rather than ignoring them. He may comment: "You haven't had much to say on that one, Paul. How are you feeling about it?" or "I sense that you wanted to disagree with Kathy, but didn't get a chance. Is there anything that you would like to discuss?" Whether in a meeting of the entire team, or in small groups of two or three, or one-on-one, the leader has an important facilitative role to play. He must be tuned in to nonverbal responses and probe if he senses that anything important is not out in the open.

The extent to which this action changes behavior and increases openness depends upon:

- *The leader's style.* Both statements above can be expressed in such a way as to create a safe and comfortable environment where the team member feels that he can respond. They can also, however, be voiced defensively or accusatively, neither of which is likely to elicit a productive response.
- *The consistency with which the leader probes.* A team member when asked if he has anything he wants to add may say no. The resistant member figures that if the leader asks for comments on two or three occasions and gets no response,

then the leader will give up and let the member return to his invisible compartment. What he doesn't bargain for is the persistence of the superior leader, who continues to probe each time he sees signs that a member isn't being open. As time passes, the resistant team member sees other members being prodded and opening up and suffering no negative consequences as a result. In most cases, when the expectation of openness is consistent, the closed member eventually begins to open up.

Creating a Safe Environment

The leader must ensure a safe environment for members who are worried about openness for personal or career reasons. Those who are holding back because of personal risk need to be listened to respectfully and protected from potential attacks by other team members. Those who are closed because of perceived career risks usually require evidence that this environment is indeed safe.

In order to ensure that no repercussions from openness occur, the leader needs:

- To work through in his own mind the issue of separating open comments from performance evaluation and to ensure that he is able to keep them apart.
- To define openness with the group. Some feel that honesty and openness mean: "Now I can tell people just what I think of them." This destructive openness is obviously not the aim.
- To be very clear about the facts and behaviors that may negatively affect a performance appraisal. Without this clarity, individuals who were previously harmed by their honesty may now assume that any criticism relates to an earlier openness on their part.
- To develop communication ground rules. (See Workout page 91.)

The leader's final responsibility in creating openness is ensuring that team members have the skills to be open without offending. We all talk about attacking the problem not the person, but do team members know how to do it, particularly when they may feel that the problem *is* the person?

Team openness depends upon the example and expectations set by the leader, upon team members' skills, and upon an environment in which being open is not a risky venture.

Team Workouts for Developing Openness

Workout: To develop ground rules to support openness in meetings.

Background: Openness goes far beyond meetings, but its development can begin in meetings. Establishing ground rules for meetings is a good starting point. Standard ones, such as, "We don't jump on each other's ideas" or "We listen actively to each other" are useful rules to remind ourselves of, to apply, and to measure our meeting behaviors against. Ground rules, however, can be much more useful if built on after a team has been working together for some time. The new ground rules which emerge will pertain specifically to any inappropriate behavior or norms recognized by team members.

Establishing ground rules gives team members the opportunity to express and come to agreement on what they believe to be the most productive behavior. Targets for ground rules are inevitably previously inappropriate behaviors, but the desired model can be described without personal reference to individuals. For example, if one individual consistently monopolizes meetings, one ground rule in all likelihood would read: "We all participate equally in meetings" or perhaps "We each take care not to monopolize meetings."

Steps:
1. Introduce the concept of ground rules and explain their purpose.
2. Ask members to individually write down one or two ground rules which they feel would be appropriate on their note pads.
3. Have members share their proposed ground rules in round-robin fashion and list them on a flipchart or blackboard.
4. Discuss each ground rule considering:
   i) Would this make our meetings more effective or more open;
   ii) If so, do we all agree to live up to it?
5. Make a final decision on the selection of ground rules.
6. Discuss and make a decision on how the ground rules will be used.

Workout: To develop ground rules to support open team communication.

Background: Ground rules that apply outside meetings can assist in carrying openness from the meeting room to the shop floor, office, or field. Teams that are suffering from a lack of openness usually consider their core issue to be ineffective communication.

Steps: The same steps for developing meeting ground rules can be used for developing team communication ground rules. If team members are inexperienced and have difficulty identifying ground rules, the facilitator may help them by suggesting they complete a sentence such as, "We would communicate more effectively if . . . " or "If we are to communicate more effectively we must . . . "

Notes for Facilitators:
- Ground rules are only platitudes if not measurable. For example, "We don't bring in hidden agendas" is a good ground rule in theory, but not measurable and observable. How then can the team ensure the ground rule is followed? Instead, the team might come to agreement on not bringing in hidden agendas and as a ground rule state, "It's okay to probe if hidden agendas are perceived."
- Ground rules are useful only if applied. They must be frequently reviewed and most importantly the team must assess how well it is living up to the ground rules.

Workout: To work through the issues when openness is lacking.

Background: This workout is designed for teams that have come to the recognition that to some extent their lack of openness is preventing them from fulfilling their potential. It takes the form of a mini-questionnaire and discussion. It can help identify underlying causes when the element of openness is weak. It helps team members assess their fear of taking risks and to what extent that fear is founded in fact.

Steps:
1. Have team members complete the following questionnaire.

Evaluation for Assessing Openness

We have agreed that we do not have the degree of openness in our team that we believe is required if we are to reach our potential. Being open in a group can be perceived as taking a risk. This brief questionnaire to be completed anonymously will help us assess why we are not sufficiently open.

Please answer each of the following questions as candidly as possible.

1. I have previously suffered repercussions from being open.　　　　　Yes ☐　　　No ☐

2. If yes, which of the following most closely describes your experience?
   - ☐　I was criticized.
   - ☐　My position was jeopardized.
   - ☐　It resulted in interpersonal conflict.
   - ☐　Other, briefly describe.

3. I fear the following might happen (you may check more than one):
   - ☐　I might look foolish.
   - ☐　I won't get support from others.
   - ☐　I will be criticized.
   - ☐　I might suffer later repercussions if a "grudge" is held.
   - ☐　I might jeopardize my career or performance rating.

2. Compile the data from the responses.
3. Share the output and discuss.

Note to Facilitator: Ensure that an anonymous and impersonal tone is maintained when sharing the output. For example, "For the most part we do not seem to be concerned about suffering repercussions, however the fear of not getting support from others was frequently highlighted." The sharing of the output and the discussion should help team members to dispel unfounded fears. It should also identify any fears that are found that indicate a need for changes within the team.

4. Develop solutions and commitments to action. Have the group discuss, "What can we do to alleviate our fears?" From these recommended solutions, develop commitments to action.

Team Fitness Element 3
COHESIVENESS

7

The Essence of Teamwork

On rare, remarkable occasions, a team just happens. Cohesiveness is spontaneous. The right group of people with the right chemistry and skills comes together with the right leader and is faced by the right challenges at the right time. Anyone who has ever been part of that sort of team experience remembers it nostalgically as a highlight in his or her life. A certain amount of euphoria is usually experienced. There is a team high. This type of cohesive experience, like other highs and euphoric experiences, can usually be sustained for a comparatively short period of time.

Spontaneous cohesion is often dependent upon a tenuous mix of elements. As new elements are introduced into the group, the cohesion dissipates, and members feel a sense of loss when things change. Group members ask, "What has happened to our team? Why can't we be the way we used to be?"

In most of our daily team experiences, the magical mix of elements is not automatically present, and we have to set about developing a method for creating cohesiveness. Cohesiveness is more than a critical element of a fit team. It is the essence of one. Without cohesiveness, members have no sense of belonging. Indeed, they have nothing to belong to.

Teams in many ways can be compared to individuals. They are made up of body and spirit, and both must be in proper working order for the entity to thrive. The body of a team consists of its mandate, tasks, goals, and objectives: *what* the team is in place to do. A team when asked who it is might respond accounting or sales. But this is not *who* it is, but *what* it is. The spirit of a team defines who it is. The spirit consists of the team's philosophy, its values, and beliefs. These work values determine how the team works and differentiate this accounting or sales team from any other accounting or sales team. In order for cohesiveness to exist, team members must agree about what they are here to do and how they believe they should do it.

Agreement about a team's mandate is usually easier to come to than agreement about a common philosophy, but on its own it is not enough. A human body can physically function, but without a strong spirit it lacks the incentive and spark to live to its fullest. Team members who agree on what they are in place to do can get the job done and meet minimum requirements, but without spirit, their team does not excel.

Superior teams come to agreement on *what* they are in place to do and *how* they should do it. But cohesiveness always requires that agreement be arrived at without losing the individual differences that make a team unique and give it its edge. The degree of cohesiveness attained depends upon the degree of commitment to that agreement.

A cohesive group is similar to an orchestra. Each member is working in the same spirit and fulfilling the same mandate, but each is contributing very separately and distinctively. Each is very clear about the part of the score he is playing. Each is using different skills, tools, and techniques, but at the same time they are all in concert.

Coming to Agreement on What the Team Does

Agreement on what a team does requires that its mandate and goals be clarified, and that team members understand and agree to the role they must play in fulfilling them.

The degree of commitment to roles and goals depends upon several factors:

- *The amount of information shared.* Open sharing on the part of the leader and the organization about all of the *w*'s related to the mandate and goals — that is, what, when, where, who, and very importantly, why — increases the employee's level of commitment. If we want trust and commitment from our team members, leaders must show them trust and respect.

Information in organizations is the major source of power. The open sharing of that power can send a powerful message. In the traditional organization, information is doled out sparingly, with careful thought as to who will be the deserving few who are trusted with it. "Let's keep this one quiet" is a frequent closing remark in rigid organizations. One disgruntled employee, tired of being in the dark, scrawled on the daily menu outside of the staff cafeteria, "Let's keep this one quiet."

Generally, the greater the openness about what is expected, what will happen, and why, the greater the individual's commitment to organizational and team goals.

- *Participation in the development of a team's mandate and goals.* The amount of involvement possible in establishing a team's mandate and goals can depend on one or a combination of factors, including the nature of the group, the level within the organization, the level of skill within the group, and the extent to which the organization itself is a participative one.

  The more that members are involved in developing goals and objectives, the greater their ownership of them. When members cannot participate in the development of the goals, sharing decisions on how the goals can be met also develops the ownership and commitment that are essential to cohesiveness.

- *The degree to which the team's goals and the individual's personal goals mesh.* If in contributing to the team, the individual has little or no opportunity to fulfill important personal goals, little likelihood exists that the individual will demonstrate a strong commitment toward the team's goals.

  Team leaders who are skilled at developing cohesiveness make a point of spending time with each team member to identify and discuss his or her personal goals. They make a concerted effort to find ways, often creative ones, of assisting that individual in fulfilling his or her personal goals while he or she is working along with the team toward its greater goals.

A personal goal may be to demonstrate a particular skill, to develop a particular aptitude into a skill, to move into a more senior position, or to increase earnings. If the personal goal is important to the individual and the present goals and position of the team offer no opportunity for fulfilling it, the individual is in the wrong place. However skilled he or she may be and whatever he or she may have to offer the team, it is unlikely this potential contribution will be realized.

Whenever possible, the astute leader redirects the member whose needs can't be fulfilled within the team to another team, department, or organization. The leader replaces him or her with someone who wants something that can be obtained by contributing to the meeting of the team's goals. Even if this person's skills are not quite as strong, the challenge and satisfaction of his or her personal accomplishments will make the person a strong contributing member.

Cohesiveness, then, depends upon a consistent understanding of the team's mandate and a commitment on the part of each team member to fulfilling it. The other requirement is agreement on team identity.

Coming to Agreement on Identity

Once teams agree upon and commit to goals and roles, they have identified *what* they are. Groups that are cohesive also know *who* they are; they have an identity. Who they are depends upon how they believe what they do should be done. Whether they or anyone else knows who they are depends upon the consistency with which they demonstrate their beliefs.

Too often the only evidence of who a group is or what it believes is hanging on the wall in an expensively framed philosophy statement. In some consistent, persistent, and focused organizations, the values from the philosophy statements which took so much time and effort to create have been operationalized and so do make the difference. In these cases, work-unit teams have made the core corporate values their own.

Consistent demonstration of corporate values contributes to team identity and cohesiveness, but teams also have separate identities made up of work values and norms that pertain only to their particular work group. It is here that the root of team dysfunction is often found.

The health-care staff of a long-term-care unit was suffering from interpersonal conflicts and low morale. The group came together in an effort to increase its teamwork effectiveness. The group was made of several nurses as well as two phys-iotherapists who spent some of their time on the long-term-care unit and the rest of their time in other parts of the hospital.

One issue examined in the team-development process was that of work values and beliefs. Since this was a long-term-care unit, patients were not there to be cured and sent home. Con-sequently, the team's basic belief was in "the quality of life." They believed in the importance of spending time with each patient, giving each one individual attention, and making each moment as rich and enjoyable as possible. Most team mem-bers contributed enthusiastically to the discussion of what they believed and how they could better demonstrate that belief.

One therapist, however, who had been quite participative in other discussions, became quiet. She gradually edged her chair back from the group and soon was sitting almost outside the group as an observer. Her discomfort was obvious. When probed for her reaction to the discussion, she displayed a good deal of courage.

"I realize," she said, "that our values and their inconsistent demonstration are the major source of our problems, and my attitude toward them has contributed to the problem. I intellec-tually accept the value of quality of life and giving each patient caring and individual attention, but I have difficulty demon-strating it. I became a physiotherapist to make people better. Here that is not going to happen. As a result, I spend as little time as possible with each patient so that I can get somewhere else where the values are closer to my own. I know others resent this and that my behavior contributes to conflict within the group."

Achieving verbal agreement with work values is usually quite easy since values are often expressed as motherhood statements. Most members of a health-care team would have difficulty saying, "I don't agree with improving the quality of life for our patients." Yet each individual may demonstrate that belief quite differently and contribute to the quality of life of the patients to varying degrees. When work values which are seen as important and in which people take pride are not consistently demonstrated, the potential for conflict exists.

Team values may be very closely tied to the task itself as in the example cited above. But equally and sometimes more important to cohesiveness are work values related to how we work with each other. Again, agreement is easier to express than to demonstrate. Teamwork values that teams often identify include commitment, supporting one another, participation, respect for one another, and honesty in relationships. The challenge here lies in both demonstration and definition.

One team was struggling with the value of commitment to job excellence and to the team. In theory, they had all agreed that it was important, but in practice, what did it mean? If some people spent time on personal telephone calls, did that mean they were not committed? If someone did not choose to attend team lunches or another did not work overtime because she had to pick up a child from daycare, were they less committed than their colleagues?

Individual differences within teams have always been a challenge to team cohesiveness. However, as our teams become increasingly disparate, the challenge grows. Disagreement and conflict in the demonstration of work values exist in all types of teams and at all levels of the organization.

A senior management team recognized that they were not working effectively together. When they examined their work values, they realized that they were their source of dysfunction. They had agreed that participation was important. Some managers made a consistent attempt to involve the right people in the right issues, but others slipped back into their traditional style and made decisions on their own or involved some people but overlooked other important contributors. Those managers who were taking the time and effort to be participative were frustrated that their commitment was not displayed by everyone. They had difficulty supporting decisions that hadn't been made participatively and put them mentally at the bottom of their priority list. This created greater conflict, because the managers who had made the decisions felt that they were not being supported, but did not understand why.

Another management group had agreed on the perennially tough issue of putting the welfare of the total organization ahead of their own territories. When some managers did not follow through, however, their colleagues felt betrayed. They questioned why they should compromise and make sacrifices when others were taking all they could get.

Teams that lack cohesiveness can benefit by stopping to assess their work values. This includes defining their values and how they should be demonstrated. From this type of team workout, members gain two benefits:

- A better understanding of each other; and
- Standards by which the team agrees to function.

Once a group is able consistently to demonstrate agreement on goals, roles, standards, and practices, a cohesive team has been developed.

8

Avoiding the Pitfalls

Clarifying Expectations:
A Quick Tonic for Team Lethargy

Like individuals, teams have very distinct personalities and become despondent and dispirited when expectations are not met. Clarifying expectations can greatly enhance cohesiveness.

When teams lament their lack of spirit, morale, or zest, members usually have a list of unfulfilled expectations. Some of the unfulfilled expectations are big issues and often to a great degree uncontrollable, such as senior management support or funding. But the items that cause the most grief and eat away at team morale are the little things. Often team members walk around with their own secret wish list and assume that somehow those expectations will be fulfilled.

"I shouldn't have to ask for help when I'm overloaded. I expect others to be sensitive enough to help when necessary," one frustrated team member complained. What is a perfectly obvious and reasonable expectation to one person may never occur to someone else or may even seem entirely unreasonable to another individual.

Spirited teams that function at a high performance level have clear expectations. Their expectations are usually made clear by having team members come together to list and examine them. When teams function effectively, expectations are:

Articulated
Clarified
Given a reality test
and, if realistic,
agreed to.

Clarifying expectations can be a very quick working tonic for teams that are not fulfilling their potential and is applicable to all types of groups: committees, work units, management teams, multi-disciplinary teams, and so on. The types of issues identified by examining expectations will, of course, differ depending on the team's place within the organization, its mandate, and its level of development. The benefits, however, are consistent.

Clarifying expectations:

- Allows team members an opportunity to address unfulfilled expectations without personalizing them (pet peeves are positively and productively aired);
- Allows for open discussion of issues previously undiscussed;
- Results in increased understanding (may explain why expectations aren't met, how perceptions differ, and produce the recognition that certain expectations are unrealistic);
- Expectations agreed to in effect become ground rules for the team. *A group of individuals can't be expected to play as a team without agreed-upon ground rules*;
- Establishes the underlying expectation that open communication will be the norm.

If the process of clarifying expectations is to help sustain the team in the long term, the expectations must be kept alive. A member of a group which was not functioning well once complained that clarifying expectations and developing ground rules were a waste of time. Her team had spent a whole day developing a long list, and nothing had changed. When asked when her group had last looked at its list, she shrugged. "Well, the day we developed it."

Tips for Leaders or Facilitators

1. Keep your list to a reasonable length. If you agree to meet too many expectations, none will be met effectively.
2. Check your expectations regularly on a "how-are-we-doing" basis. If your list is a short one — five or less — you may

check each one. If longer, highlight a couple of expectations at each meeting. The frequency with which you monitor your agreed-upon expectations will depend upon the need of the team.

3. If as facilitator of the process you feel that the team members may have difficulty getting started, you can ask them, after your preamble, to complete the sentence, "I expect myself and my team members to . . . " This process usually results in the clarification of expectations relating to behaviors. However, role clarification is another important aspect in meeting expectations.

A lab team suffering from low morale and high absenteeism decided that the appointment of a new manager provided the prime opportunity for a team-development session. This manager was to be the third in just over a year. The first manager, Margaret, had been with the group for several years. Kathleen had spent about a year with them, and now Doreen was being appointed. As part of the development session, Doreen and the lab staff were asked to clarify their expectations of each other.

Staff members quickly and consistently identified one expectation that they had of Doreen. "We expect you to work part time on the bench with us like Margaret did, so you can understand our problems." The ensuing discussion revealed that their last manager had not worked beside them part time as Margaret had. She was "always in her office or off at some meeting and didn't understand our problems." It became clear why morale had plummeted during the previous year.

Doreen responded to the group by describing her role. When she was finished, the team exclaimed, "You don't have time to work beside us on the bench, do you? We didn't realize the manager's job had changed." They recognized that their expectation was unrealistic and that the management role was now a full-time one. Working alongside them was no longer part of the job. That previously unarticulated and unrealistic expectation had created a miserable environment for a year.

Clarifying expectations is a good spot check and maintenance tool for high-performance teams and an effective reenergizer for those experiencing lethargy. If members' expectations of one another are not clear, the group will lack cohesiveness. On the other hand, just as detrimental is an overdose of cohesiveness.

When Teams Have Too Much of a Good Thing

I am often struck by how consistently true is the homily about having too much of a good thing. Money, love, and success are all wonderful. Yet each, if excessive, can do greater harm than good. So too with cohesiveness. Cohesiveness, as we have said, is more than simply an *element* of an effective team. It is the *essence* of an effective team. Without it, a team has no spirit, no spark, no drive, no commitment, and no more than mediocre accomplishments. Cohesiveness, you may think, is the exception to the rule. Most leaders find it hard to imagine too much drive and too much commitment.

A clerical department decided that they would like to do some team building. They were a group of about forty people, divided fairly equally into two units: A and B. They realized that the group was too large and tasks and goals too diverse to expect to function totally as a team. They did not always depend on each other to get the job done and recognized that forty people could not share decisions.

They did, however, frequently depend upon each other in some important ways. They needed to keep each other informed about certain aspects of the job, yet this wasn't happening. They also needed to consider other parts of the department before making decisions, yet this was frequently overlooked. Morale had been low, and cliques had developed.

It was decided that it would be beneficial to spend two days together away from work to examine how the department worked together and how they could work together more effectively.

Unit A saw themselves as having already developed a team. They felt positive about their own unit, but did not feel as positive about their relations with members of the rest of the department. Unit A had a leader who was enthusiastic, committed, and who believed in teamwork. The members of his unit, for the most part, followed his lead.

On Day One of the teamwork effectiveness session, the department was divided into subgroups that mixed A and B unit members to discuss strengths, issues, and opportunities for improvement. Throughout the day Unit A members enthusiastically gave examples of what they did as a group and why they worked so effectively together.

At dinner that evening, Unit A arrived as a group, dressed in matching hats and T-shirts with The A Team printed on the back of each. They did not receive the positive reception that they expected, and the following morning the group demonstrated more stress and conflict than before the session had begun.

Day Two was a challenging day of addressing what Unit B saw as the major block to departmental unity, effectiveness, and morale: elitism on the part of Unit A. Unit B believed the other group saw themselves as superior and perfect. In the view of Unit B, the members of Unit A flaunted their superiority in such a way that the rest of the department felt that they could never fit in or measure up. Unit A was a prime example of too much of a good thing.

As a team's cohesiveness develops, so does its sense of identity and pride in its accomplishments. This pride can give a team its energy and its edge on performance. Pride, however, became Unit A's downfall. It gave the unit's members the illusion of being nearly perfect. With this sense of perfection, the team stopped examining itself for flaws or opportunities for improvement. In their excitement about their own success, team members lost their sensitivity to others outside their group. They could have been a positive model for the whole department, but they missed their opportunity. Instead of sharing their team spirit, they hoarded it. As a result, instead of being respected, they were rejected.

In this case, two distinct teams were attempting to develop greater teamwork effectiveness within the larger group and were hindered by an overdose of team spirit. Individual teams, however, can also suffer the side effects of over-cohesiveness, if they are not monitored well. These are some potential pitfalls that strong cohesive teams should watch for.

Lack of Self-Critiquing

Groups that are working well often feel no need to stop and check how they are doing. They know they are excelling. Consequently, when the occasion arises for self-evaluation, they often find it difficult to look at themselves with sufficient objectivity to identify potential problems. Cracks aren't noticed until they become gaping holes, and people moan, "What happened to our team?"

To ensure that it is indeed as sound as it feels, a strong cohesive group must stop periodically to examine itself and would probably benefit from having assistance from someone outside the team. A person sufficiently distanced from the team may recognize potential problems that members are too close to see. A strong facilitator can also assist in challenging team members to look at themselves objectively and can provide the structure within which they can do so effectively.

An Illusion of Cohesiveness

When this happens, a core team often exists within a larger group. These members usually feel very good about themselves and the team and are usually confident, outgoing individuals who have developed a strong culture based on a job well executed and on having fun. They have developed strong group norms, have their own sense of humor, and patterns of interrelating. Their social structure is often marked by "in" jokes or nicknames. They are usually a hard-working and affirmative group.

Their assumption is that because they personally feel part of the team, that their work unit is indeed a team. Because they are a vocal, confident, and positive group, that image is projected. It is not uncommon for a group that is dysfunctional in many ways to project an image of a cohesive team. The leader believes he has a team, the most influential group members believe they are a team, and outsiders often believe they are seeing a team at work.

What isn't recognized is that a fringe group may exist who are feeling very differently. They usually do not fit in socially with the more vociferous core group and often feel uncomfortable. They believe the power group takes over and makes all of the decisions, which most of the time is an accurate perception. They do not feel part of the team. Indeed, they feel very isolated and less than good about themselves and the group as a whole. Although they may have criticisms of many aspects of the team, they do not feel free to express their concerns. This results from a variety of conditions and experiences, as well a personal traits of the fringe group members.

- They may fear that any suggestion that the team is not perfect will be considered a poor attitude or non-support.
- The influential core group may hear but ignore as untrue or unimportant any criticism raised.
- The "aren't we great" culture may be so strong that suggesting anything different requires taking a great risk.
- Fringe members often are quieter, less assertive individuals than core-group members and don't have the skills to influence the more dominant core group.
- The leader often identifies with the core group and is proud of his team. He may talk a great deal about what a great team he has. Fringe members may be hesitant to suggest to him that what he is so proud of just does not exist.

How can a leader misread his group so badly? Even relatively strong leaders have fallen into this trap. Teams that suffer from an illusion of cohesiveness typically have leaders who:

- Are outgoing, enthusiastic, and very much want a team to evolve. When they see positive signs, they are eager to accept them as a confirmation of success.
- Have a personal style that is much closer to that of the core-group members. They relate more comfortably to them, spend more time with them, and as a result receive their informal information from them. The news they hear is all good.
- Recognize, and justly so, that not all team members are going to be equally vociferous and equally participative and assume that the fringe group members are simply quieter. It never occurs to these leaders that these members might be dissatisfied. They can't understand how anyone could be dissatisfied when she is a member of such a great team.

Overlooking problems when appearances are good is an easy error to make. Managers are busy people, they count their blessings when things appear to be going well, and generally don't look for problems if none appear to exist.

The superior leader, however, is vigilant. She maintains her objectivity and sensitivity and checks the team's climate periodically. She makes a point of staying in touch with the quieter group members. She celebrates successes and shares the enthusiasm but also objectively checks the reality of appearances to ensure that no fringe group exists.

The fringe group may be several outsiders or one or two disenfranchised individuals. If a group requires a scapegoat, it is inevitably a member of the fringe group who is designated. The leader of the fit team, however, ensures that all team members are protected.

A healthy cohesive team is able to capitalize on individual differences. Team members may hold very different points of view, express them openly, and yet effectively come to consensus.

Team Workouts for Developing Cohesiveness

Workout: To check consistency of understanding of purpose. To develop a common focus.

Steps: Bring team members together.
1. Ask each to complete the statement "The purpose (mandate/primary goal) of our team is..."
2. Share statements.
3. Discuss any differences in interpretation.
4. As a group, develop and come to agreement on a statement of purpose.

Workout: To develop team identity.

Steps: Bring team members together.
1. Ask team members to identify "what makes us unique."
2. Discuss the elements identified.
3. Have team members choose:
   (i) the elements they believe are most consistently evident in the team;
   (ii) those that are not as consistently evident.
4. Have the team identify how the members can increase the consistency of the weaker elements.
5. Develop commitments for specific improvements as required.

Workout: To clarify expectations.

Steps: Bring team members together.
1. Ask team members individually to list their expectations of their team members.

or

Ask them to complete the statement, "In order to make this an even more effective team, I expect myself and others to . . ."
2. Have team members share their expectations. (List expectations on a flipchart or board.)
3. Discuss whether each is fair and realistic.
4. For those the team agrees are fair and realistic, discuss:
   • which do we already fulfill.
   • which do we need to work on.
5. For those that require work, ask team members to make specific commitments to action.

Workout: To measure and increase cohesiveness.

Steps:
1. Ask team members to complete the Team Fitness Test. (See Chapter 1.)
2. Share the results of the questionnaire.
3. Recognize and celebrate your strengths.
4. Discuss in particular those statements that received inconsistent responses.
5. Develop commitments to action for any elements which require development.

Note: Widely different responses can indicate the presence of a core and fringe group.

Team Fitness Element 4
CHANGE
COMPATIBILITY

9

Responding to Change

"Change is the only thing that is permanent."

Heraclitus, sixth century B.C.

Since the Industrial Revolution, employees in plants and corporate hallways have quipped with an air of cleverness and originality, "The only thing constant around here is change!"

We have not changed. We continue to recognize the permanence of change, perhaps with a little more apprehension. Change has become a buzz word, and we spend a good deal of time talking about it. We talk about the Impetus for Change, Change Agents, the Stress of Change, and Resistance to Change. Futurists, such as Alvin Toffler, have been the catalysts for a more intense examination of change. But — as the history of our organizations frequently demonstrates — we enjoy the intellectual pursuit, but tend to be either reluctant or too lethargic to apply the insights that we gain. As a result, "Too little too late" is a frequent organizational post-mortem comment.

Failing to apply what we know has been our corporate Achilles' heel. Until recently, we managed to limp along in spite of it. Now, with slimmer resources and the increased pace and magnitude of change, many cannot keep up. For those organizations that are falling behind, this may be the last chance to apply what they know. By now, organizations should know that in order to survive, let alone thrive, they must learn to manage change better. They should know that when a change fails, it most often does so due to human factors. They should know that the organizations that will be the most successful in the next frenetic five to twenty years will be those with a high change-compatibility. And finally, they should know that increasing that compatibility means increasing the flexibility, responsiveness, and change-management skills of the teams that must assimilate change and make it work.

Flexibility is not easily taught. Increasing flexibility usually means changing long-term rigid behavior. In order to be flexible, a team must be open, cohesive, skilful, must have the opportunity to participate and recognize the responsibility in productive participation, and, finally, must be responsive to change.

The way in which groups respond to change is a significant reflection of their level of team fitness.

The Rigid Group

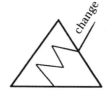

The change and/or the group are damaged.

The rigid group avoids change, particularly that which is not of its own making. When change is imposed, it is inflexible and cannot bend. When this happens, something gets broken. Either damage is done to the group, usually through stress of change, or the change itself seldom materializes as was originally envisaged. Internally, the group suffers from its own resistance to the change. In a classic case, negative attitudes abound. Group members are on the alert for evidence that indeed the change won't work as they have proclaimed. They focus on the problems and ignore any signs of success. Conversations dwell on anything that they believe confirms that their work world is in a terrible state. Each negative response elicits another negative response and morale plummets. Conflicts arise as group members, stressed and depressed, find fault not only with "them" — whoever imposed the change — but with each other. In particular, conflict arises if any group members make an effort to support the change.

Many team members suffer personally from the stress of working in a negative environment and perhaps, in addition, from fear of the change. Will I be able to learn the new job? Can I adjust? Will there still be a place for me? are common concerns. This stress, if maintained over a period of time, can affect the individual physically and emotionally. This is transferred to the group as increased absenteeism, a drop in quality or productivity, increased conflict, and low morale. Ultimately, the rigid group is severely damaged.

The Limp Group

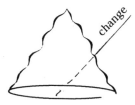

The change doesn't take.

The limp group may complain, but it doesn't usually actively resist. Members impassively accept the change, but do not embrace it. In the limp group, the change either "doesn't take" or the change doesn't work as envisaged. Comments such as "Didn't we put a new procedure in place a while ago that was supposed to look after that?" are common in the limp group.

Change can also create dis-ease in the limp group. When the limp group suffers, it is not as much from the stress of the change, as from stress created by the recognition that members' attempts to implement change are seldom effective and they aren't able to come to grips with why. Lack of clear guidelines and direction result in frustration and anxiety.

The Flexible Team

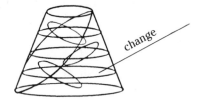

The change is assimilated.

The flexible team responds positively to change. It does an objective assessment of an upcoming change. That assessment includes the following types of questions:

- Is this a good change?
- If yes, how can we make it work?
- If no, do we have the power to change it or the influence to have it reexamined?
- If yes, how should we go about it?
- If no, how can we do our best to make it work and demonstrate an affirmative attitude, even though it is not a change we would have chosen?

Flexible teams see change as a constant. They recognize that even a well-managed change is seldom "written in stone" and may undergo many variations and redirectives between inception and implementation.

Increasing Team Flexibility

Occasionally change compatibility does not have to be developed. This happens when a team is made up of a group of flexible individuals, each of whom is affirmative, is sufficiently self-confident to prevent the change from being viewed as a personal threat, and who can objectively assess and integrate change.

In most cases, however, a team has a mix of individuals. Individuals demonstrate many of the same characteristics as groups. Although they may not demonstrate all of the characteristics of a given group, most can recognize themselves as predominantly flexible, rigid, or limp.

The Rigid Individual

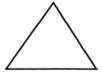

Characteristics:
- requires structure
- enjoys routine
- has a one-thing-at-a-time approach to work
- is detail oriented
- relies on facts and figures (proof)
- prefers low-risk situations
- prefers task to process
- would rather do it than talk about it

Change compatibility
- low
- demonstrates resistance to change

The Limp Individual

Characteristics:
- dislikes rigid routine and structure
- creative
- thrives on communication
- relies on intuition
- is receptive to risk
- rates interpersonal relationships as critical to job satisfaction
- prefers process to task
- would rather talk about it than do it
- does not demonstrate follow-through ability

Change compatibility
- low if required to follow through
- is receptive to change but does not have the skills to make a change work

The Flexible Individual (The Supreme Balancer)

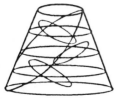

Characteristics:
- demonstrates a good mix and balance of task and process, ideas and logic, people's and organization's needs
- objectively evaluates change
- has strong planning and problem-solving skills

Change compatibility
- high

Both rigid and limp individuals demonstrate characteristics that can be strengths during the process of a change. If too much of a good thing exists, however, the strengths become weaknesses. For example, some individuals have so great a need for structure that they cannot perform without it or, to take another example, some individuals place so much emphasis on developing new ideas that they never follow them through. In these cases, the individuals' strengths become weaknesses.

Rigid individuals, because of their resistance to change, pose the most obvious threat. Some individuals are rigid by nature; many have been conditioned to demonstrate rigid characteristics. Our organizations have been built on and by the characteristics of rigid men and women. People traditionally have been hired, rewarded, and promoted on their ability to work effectively in structured environments, to follow instructions and procedures, to duplicate details, and to make sure things continue to be done the way they have always been done. Many have learned their lessons well and are now having difficulty accepting that what worked yesterday, or at least what we were able to get by with, no longer is sufficient for today.

The rigid individual is often seen as negative. He is the first to say something won't work, may say no before considering a proposal, and believes that if "that's the way we've always done it, it must be right."

Some rigid individuals of course are negative. However, for the most part when individuals resist change, it's a defense mechanism. They are consciously or unconsciously trying to avoid a situation which is at least uncomfortable and probably threatening to them. They feel they risk little by saying no, but they fear where yes or tell me more might lead.

Some individuals have been rigid for so long and so determinedly that they may never be able to become sufficiently flexible to thrive in today's organization or team. Some are simply badly arthritic; others are better described as fossilized and are definitely "set in their ways." For most, however, an opportunity for growth exists. Change compatibility can be developed if individuals are supported and an effort is made to meet their needs in the process.

Resistance to a particular change develops most often very early in the process; most commonly in fact at the announcement stage. The effective communication of a change is vital to preventing resistance. Communication about an upcoming change should be *early, planned, personal, positive, participative*, and *ongoing*.

Early Communication (Beating the Grapevine)

The first law of communicating change effectively is to beat that most efficient organizational communication line, the grapevine. In most organizations, it would be better named the sour grapevine because it picks up, invents if necessary, and quickly spreads damaging rumors about any anticipated change. We all know that it functions with a speed unparalleled by even the organization's automated communication systems.

The grapevine has the unfair advantage of being able to develop within the employee population strongly unfavorable attitudes toward a project which is still in its infancy and unable to prove its worthiness. This negativism, often based on misperceptions and nonfactual information, is difficult to reverse. Rumor from colleagues is somehow always more believable than facts from management.

The only way to short-circuit the grapevine is to ensure that as much factual information as possible is presented as early as possible. Contrary to this rule, management often waits as long as possible to announce a pending change.

Some managers ask, "Isn't it potentially harmful to announce something that may not be completely finalized? Won't it hurt management credibility if we change course after announcing a direction?" The reality is that a change will be announced in one way or another. If management doesn't announce it, the rumor mill will. Employees may have no specific information, but at the very least they will know that "something is going on" in all of those meetings behind closed doors, and if secrecy surrounds it, the consensus is that it can't be good news. And each rumor spread in elevators, at water coolers, and over coffee cements another block in a wall of resistance. If this wall is well built before a formal announcement is made, it can be very difficult to win commitment to the change or even alleviate resistance.

In addition to short-circuiting the grapevine, announcing change as early as possible also gives people a chance to adjust to the idea before it becomes a reality. Change shock, caused by too much change too fast, can then be lessened.

Planned Communication

The flexible organization reverses traditional thinking. Instead of, "What do we want them [the employees] to know?" they ask, "What do they need to know if they are to participate positively in the change process?"

In this one question they are recognizing that, a) the initial announcement can be more than a necessary downward communiqué. It offers a prime opportunity to win a commitment to the change; and b) people have a right to as much information as possible about anything that is going to affect them. Planning the communication of a change also includes predicting team members' objections and deciding how to handle them. Often a change agent's most effective approach is to acknowledge possible objections early in his presentation. "I recognize that some of you may be concerned about . . . " When the leader does not do this, objections are often raised by team members after the positive aspects of the change have been presented. This can result in the leader appearing to have been put on the defensive. Where members do not feel free to be honest, objections may go unspoken (at least in the meeting) and an opportunity to lessen or eliminate the concern may be lost.

Personal Communication

Managers often avoid announcing changes in person. Writing a memo is shorter than the process of making an announcement, and it avoids the necessity of dealing with hostile reactions.

Ronald Lippitt said there is no such thing as resistance. There is only legitimate concern. While we may not agree entirely with this statement, we all know of instances when unaddressed concern has led to resistance.

A personal announcement gives employees an opportunity to express their concerns or to ask for clarification. It can also ensure that the message is not misinterpreted and that a positive tone is set for the process of change.

Positive Communication

Being positive is probably the greatest dilemma for leaders who do not agree with an imposed change, but are required to act as the change agent and make it work. For a leader to pretend to be enthusiastic about a change with which he doesn't agree is difficult, insincere, and ineffective. To walk around trying to sell the change on a "this-is-the-greatest-idea-ever" basis obviously would not work, and yet if a leader does not approach a change with a supportive attitude, the chances of its success are slim.

His supportiveness then must lie in focusing not on the change itself, but on making it work and consistently demonstrating his commitment to the success of implementing the change. Commitment is essential to a successful change. Commitment is contagious, and it can be best spread by the leader. This is illustrated in the following example.

An organization planning a restructuring of a department invited recommendations from each of the department's units. When the final decision was made, the restructuring plan did not match the recommendations of all of the units. Three in particular had made recommendations which were very different from the final results. Each supervisor was told that all input had been appreciated and had been carefully considered and that the decision presented was final. Each of the unit supervisors presented the change to the people reporting to them at a unit meeting.

Unit A

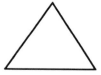

The supervisor opened the meeting. "Well, you people aren't going to like what I've got to tell you . . . "

Once the decision had been described by the supervisor, the discussion focused on why the policy wouldn't work, how their recommendation had been superior, and how management never listened. The discussion ended with a comment from one of the team members, "We know this won't work and we'll prove it to them."

Unit B

The supervisor began the meeting with, "Well, I'm afraid management didn't go with our idea . . . "

An hour-long discussion included why the policy wouldn't work, why management hadn't accepted their recommendation, and how Unit D, whose recommendations had been incorporated in the policy, was always favored. A good deal of time was also spend on whether they should rework and resubmit their recommendation. The meeting ended with the comment, "Well, I guess we'll have to live with it."

Unit C

The supervisor began the meeting. "I have management's final decision on the reorganization. I will read it to you shortly. First, I want to explain what the decision was based on . . . "

When one or two members began to criticize the decision, the supervisor quickly intervened. "Look, we've had our kick at the can. Our input was considered, this is a final decision, a fait accompli. Let's not waste our time and energy looking at what's wrong with it. I'd like us to use the rest of our time planning how we can make it work."

Participative Communication

People must be involved appropriately in changes that affect them. As discussed in the section on Productive Participation, the right people should be involved at the right level of participation. It is important, then, to consider before the initial communication of the change to what extent individuals can participate in the change and the decisions around it and how.

Ongoing Communication

"There, that's done. We have communicated" is frequently how managers react after announcing a change. But the initial meeting should be only the beginning, particularly if a change is an important one. The most important time to communicate is when nothing obvious is happening. It is then that the momentum and support initially built can wane, and negativism move in. It can take some creativity to find something to communicate when nothing is happening, but people should be informed that the proposal is still on track; they should be reminded of the benefits and opportunities; and they need to receive any information that is available on the change no matter how unimportant it may appear.

Increasing Change Compatibility

A team's change compatibility can be increased by assisting individuals in developing greater receptivity to change for rigid members and by putting systems in place to ensure follow-through for limp members.

Change compatibility is increased when:
- during the process of a change, as much structure as possible is provided for those who need it;
- individuals are provided with the information they need to participate positively in the change process. This will probably include why and how the change will affect them;
- individuals have an opportunity to participate productively in a change that affects them (as discussed in the section on Productive Participation). The adage,

"People who plan the battle don't battle the plan," has been consistently demonstrated in the management of organizational change;
- the change is paced whenever possible;
- systems are put in place to assist individuals to follow through and to ensure that the change lasts;
- individuals are provided with required training to perform any new task comfortably;
- individuals know that they are important.

The leader can do a good deal to develop increased flexibility in the members of his team, but the element of change compatibility, like all of the other fitness elements, develops most quickly and effectively when the team stops to assess its change compatibility, identifies opportunities for growth, develops commitments to action, and follows through on them.

Change compatibility to a great extent is a matter of attitude. Fit teams that thrive on change recognize that, "It's not what happens to us in life that counts, so much as how we respond to what happens to us."

Team Workouts for Developing Change Compatibility

Workout: To increase your team's change compatibility.

Steps:
1. Consider each of the statements in the box above.
   To what extent is each action or situation present in your team during changes?
2. Identify opportunities for improvement.
3. Develop commitments to action for increasing your team's change compatibility.

Workout: To reduce or prevent resistance to change.

Steps:
1. Consider each of the criteria for the effective communication of change. A change should be:

   - Announced early
   - Planned
   - Personal
   - Presented positively
   - Participative
   - Ongoing.

2. Determine which criteria are consistently met when a change is introduced in your team and which require improvement.
3. Develop commitments to action for each item identified as requiring improvement.

CURRENT TEAMWORK
CHALLENGES

10

Four-Dimensional Leadership

In a fit team, each of the four elements — productive partici-pation, openness, cohesiveness, and change compatibility — is strong. Unless the team is self-managed, the strength of these elements depends to a great extent on the leadership. Yet the job of leadership is more challenging today than it has ever been. Leaders face the challenge of managing in transition, of discarding old systems and integrating new ones. In many ways, they must manage in what Marshall McLuhan described as an "age of anxiety."

One burnt-out manager described it like this: "The people upstairs want me to do more for less; my people want to do less for more; and the systems guy wants to know why I haven't even had time to find the on button on the computer he plunked on my desk. It's a whole new ball game, and nobody has taught me the rules."

The ball game is indeed new, and the champions are using new tools and have developed new concepts. Most managers recognize the necessity of doing things differently. The frus-tration frequently expressed lies in identifying precisely *how* to do things differently; in changing our values to match the new directions, and in developing skills to make the transition.

Not only is the job of leadership tougher today than it was in the past, it is tougher than it will be in the future. The chal-lenge of managing in transition is that people, departments, and organizations are at various places on the road from the traditional to the team-focused organization. Once most of us are there, the job will be much easier.

Happily, a constantly increasing number of managers see

team-leadership practices as just common sense. Some managers, however, still resist adopting new tools. Some cite concern that we are often introduced to change for the sake of change and argue that progress is change but change for the sake of change is not progress. Others try out the new tools but aren't given enough instruction about how to use them and so meet with a good deal less than satisfactory results. And still others have the old tools so ingrained in their management behavior that they cannot change, particularly when they don't understand why the old tools are no longer working.

Traditional management style and techniques worked relatively well in an organizational world that was predictable, where both internal and external change occurred at a leisurely pace, where resources were plentiful, and where employees did not expect to be consulted on decisions that affected them. It was quite different from the world we function in today.

In that simpler world, the good manager knew almost everything that he needed to know to enable his department to meet its objectives. He had probably worked his way up through the department and had an intimate knowledge of most of the jobs. Change happened slowly so that his knowledge was credible for some time. A good manager had most of the answers to most of the questions. Participation was not as necessary for effectiveness. If productivity slipped, an easy remedy was to convert one readily available resource — dollars — into another resource — people — and so resolve the problem or at least the visible symptom.

A not-quite-so-easy remedy was to motivate employees to new heights. Although corporations spent large portions of substantial training budgets on management courses on how to motivate unmotivated employees, for the most part little changed. Managers had the sense that they had to do something either *to* or *for* the employee. They had to find the right button to push and, as the number of buttons available were as numerous as the differences between individuals, they had trouble. The old "carrot or the stick" analogy of motivating by reward or punishment was the easiest concept to understand and apply. Because concern for people had increased and because carrots were plentiful and appeared to do the job well enough, they became the most favored motivational tool.

Today's job, which is to be more competitive with less and to do so in a highly volatile, fast-paced environment, requires a very different concept of leadership. The leader can no longer personally have all of the answers; change is happening too fast for that. He doesn't have easy solutions, such as increasing his staff. Carrots are scarce as tight budgets no longer allow large bonuses or salary increases to be used as incentives; as organizations with less hierarchy provide fewer promotional opportunities; and as employees more vociferously tell us that their first priorities are not always money and career. Today's leader can no longer "make things happen," but must create the environment where the right things can happen. The leader's primary task is no longer to control, but to facilitate; no longer to motivate, but to empower individuals.

Leaders are sometimes tempted to slip back into a traditional management role because it seems much simpler. Delegating, controlling, and even motivating seem cleaner and easier than facilitating and empowering. But facilitating and empowering can be simple. Leaders must identify what needs to be done — and do it.

Today's leaders who excel are multi-dimensional beings. Each facet of their leadership is essential to their own and their team's success. Each on its own is a powerful attribute. But none on its own can create the culture that grows fit, flexible teams. The combination of four leadership dimensions results in the balance and directed energy that drives superior teams.

Leadership Dimension 1: Achieving Centeredness

All leaders face challenges: perhaps too few resources, staff conflicts, seemingly impossible deadlines. Some leaders are centered, however, and to them these types of challenges are part of the job. These leaders know they will overcome the challenges, survive, and indeed thrive.

To leaders who are not centered, these circumstances are not challenges but problems, and they are frequently overwhelming. This core of well-being within a leader results from feeling good about oneself and feeling good about the work environment he immerses himself in.

Leaders who feel good about themselves have a personal and a professional confidence. The professional confidence results from understanding their role and knowing they have the skills to fulfill it. They know what they believe about the leadership role and they know those beliefs are in sync with the modern work world. They know what they believe about what their teams should be doing and how they should be doing it. They know that this is in sync with their organization and the modern business or professional world within which they operate.

Not everyone is blessed with personal self-confidence, but once a person becomes comfortable with who he is as a leader, he becomes more comfortable about who he is as a person. The higher his level of personal confidence, however, the easier a leader can succeed within an environment with which he is not perfectly attuned.

A leader, who is unable to productively handle discrepancies between himself and his work environment, cannot develop a team. If a leader disagrees with items as major as the direction in which his organization is going, its predominant values and culture, or the management style within that culture, an organizational fit does not exist. If, for example, an organization's most cherished value is cost effectiveness but the manager's is quality, and if he believes that quality is consistently sacrificed for cost, he may feel a good deal of unease. He will have difficulty introducing cost-cutting programs to his team with any sense of real commitment.

Centeredness requires comfort in the leadership role, leadership beliefs that are in tune with today's business and professional worlds, being in sync with one's organization, and a feeling of personal commitment to, and preferably enthusiasm for, the mandate of one's team. This dimension of centeredness is frequently ignored. People often assume that not being in tune with their organization is normal or at the very least has to be lived with.

When managers recognize the need for increased team fitness, they tend to begin by looking outward at the team and its members. Instead, the place to start is at one's own professional core.

Lack of centeredness is conveyed by the attitude we present.

A new supervisor described himself as awed by the extent to which his attitude influenced those reporting to him. He recalled one morning when he arrived at the office tired and depressed, which was contrary to his usually upbeat personal style. About ten o'clock he looked up and noticed that everyone seemed to be frowning and working at half-speed. He decided that the rainy weather had put everyone in the doldrums. Around one o'clock, one of his employees came up to him and asked, "What's wrong with you today, Ken? You've got everybody down."

Everyone has a down day, but if negative feelings about the organization, the job at hand, or uncertainties about the leadership role are regularly emanating from the leader, it becomes impossible to create the spark that ignites team commitment.

Leadership Dimension 2: Focusing with Feeling

A leader can't lead if she doesn't have a destination to which she is committed. If the leader does not believe that getting there is important, that the journey itself will be exciting and the arrival fulfilling, followers soon get bored, fall by the wayside, or choose their own direction.

I frequently hear complaints that, "People today don't care. Most are nine-to-fivers. They're only here to pay the rent. They just aren't committed." In my work with teams, however, my experience is not that people don't want to be committed, but that they desperately want something worthwhile to be committed to. Most people want to believe that things can be better whether in the world or in the workplace. They want to be part of a success story. Where apathy exists, leaders lack vision or if they have it, it is not shared and people aren't given the opportunity to be part of it.

I would challenge anyone to identify a great leader who didn't have a dream of a better world or a dream of success. Our great leaders throughout history have demonstrated over and over again how a dream can pull people together like a magnet and charge them with the energy and the desire to work together toward it.

Martin Luther King's "I have a dream" speech, Winston Churchill's "We shall fight on the beaches . . . ", Kennedy's "Ask not what your country can do for you — ask what you can do for your country" all focused the attention and energy of the people they led. Each leader had his own personal vision and each was able to communicate it in such a way that it became alive in the minds and hearts of others.

Vision was driven home so well in the eighties that most leaders now recognize the need to think beyond the short term. The challenge is two-fold: leaders must not be sidetracked by the immediate issues and they must inspire their staff to become committed to their ideals.

Staying on track depends upon the leader's commitment to the long-term goal, upon planning, and upon persistence. Getting people committed requires the leader to be able to draw a picture of the ideal. The picture is not drawn on a flipchart or a board; it is drawn in the leader's mind and, if it's to be successful, in the minds and hearts of those she leads. The picture is not of targets and figures alone, but is a picture of what the team's work world will look and feel like when the ideal is fulfilled.

We know that visualizing our success greatly increases our chances of attaining it. Sports figures have always intuitively realized the benefits of mentally rehearsing their success.

Imagery has now achieved official acceptance, and many athletes and other professionals are trained in the art of visualization. It appears that the clearer, more detailed, and more precise the image that is attained, the greater our chances of experiencing it. Once the leader has a picture that sparks a feeling of excitement within herself, she knows that she has identified an ideal that she and her team can make a reality.

Introducing your vision to your team by beginning "I have a dream" may not bring you the same success that it did Martin Luther King. Although oratorical skills and charisma can be a strength in organizational leadership, a leader can demonstrate greatness without them. What is essential is that first you yourself are committed to the ideal.

Managers who demonstrate a low-key style often feel handicapped in leading a team. They feel they have neither the charismatic nor leadership qualities that develop spirit and commitment to a goal. Whatever your style, however, the people around you know when you are committed to something. Commitment when consistent is contagious.

The second essential requirement is describing your picture of the ideal in terms that team members can recognize and identify with. Telling the team that you envision doubling orders or cutting customer complaints by fifty percent is giving them something they understand, but probably can't picture and certainly can't feel. You haven't told them what it will look like; what it will feel like; in what way each of them will be part of it; and in what way each of their work lives will be different.

What would your ideal work world look like? Would there be more people? New equipment? Would the location be different? What would increased business mean in terms of activity within the office? Would the phones be ringing more regularly? Would you need extra equipment and staff to input the increased volume of new orders? Would people be responding differently? Would a letter arrive on your desk from the president thanking your team for their contribution? Would a picture of your team receiving an award from the president for outstanding achievement hang on the wall?

The manager's description of success which follows describes what I mean. The setting is a meeting of the Order and Customer Service Department, which he heads.

Paul Brown, manager: "Every phone in this office will be ringing off the hook with new orders. Cathy, you know that empty space between the window and the filing cabinet? There will be desks there for the new assistants you are going to need to man the phones.

"Mark, you know that new system you've been wanting for processing invoices that we haven't been able to cost justify? Well, we're going to need the latest and the best to handle the increase in volume you're going to see. So keep on top of everything that's coming on to the market so we'll be able to purchase when the time is right.

"Susan, you're going to have a long personal thank-you note on the top of your desk, commending you on your attention to detail, quick response time, and as always helpfulness, and guess who it's going to be signed by? Ken Francis."

(Susan and the team members laugh. Ken, the supervisor of shipping, has been giving Susan a hard time for over a month, complaining that she hasn't been giving him quick and accurate information to ensure that the customer receives the right goods on time.)

"Mary, your customer complaint line is going be so quiet, we're going to have to get you trained on something else.

"And right here on this wall is going to be a large colored photograph of the president presenting us with a special award for achievement.

"Now, how can we start making it happen?"

The focus of each picture will depend on the level within the organization at which it is being visualized. When a corporate leader has a vision for an entire organization, each team within that organization should still have its own picture of the perfect world. This picture will describe its own ideal within the context of the greater organizational vision.

The ideal becomes even more alive when team members can

share in the development of what it will look and feel like. Sharing in the development of the picture can create enormous energy which will drive the team forward toward it. However, that dream must be kept alive in everyone's mind. As it fades, so does the energy that drives the team forward. Without reinforcing reminders, the urgency of each day fills our minds, absorbs our energy, and soon crowds out the dream. Some teams keep their focus by developing a symbol of success and keeping it posted where everyone can see it. Others ensure long-term goals are kept alive by discussing them regularly at meetings.

When a leader focuses with feeling and makes everyone see and feel the picture in her mind, the energy created propels the team to success.

Leadership Dimension 3: Involving Others

Although all four team elements and all four leadership dimensions are critical, the dimension of involving people is the most instrumental in developing team fitness.

Few individuals feel or demonstrate commitment toward something that they do not feel a part of or membership in. Ownership is developed through participation. "Why doesn't she ask us?" is a frequent lament in groups that are described as lacking commitment.

Involving people sounds like one of the simplest leadership dimensions to develop. It *is* simple, but at the same time it can be deceiving. Too often managers assume its simplicity means that no thought or planning is required. You ask for people's comments, have more meetings, and let them know what is going on. All of which is correct. However, each of these requires planning, skills, and consistency.

The flexible leader shares the decision-making process. The increased sharing of decisions in the world of the flexible team is paradoxical. The team leader on one hand is decreasing her decision-making load by passing authority on to others, but at the same time she must make decisions that are sometimes more complex. Deciding whom to involve, in what, when, and how can be more difficult than deciding which tasks must be performed when, how, and by whom.

Involving people is also deceiving because it is so easily overlooked. Mark Johnston had always seen himself as a team leader and coach. He was the captain of football and hockey teams in high school and at university. After university, he became a high-school teacher and the coach of the football team.

Mark changed careers and joined an automotive-parts manufacturing firm as a salesman. His enthusiasm and social skills made sales quite easy for him, but he felt he had leadership qualities which weren't being tapped. He eventually asked for a move into management. When a manager of an administrative department came up for retirement, Mark was given the job. Mark saw this as a tremendous opportunity. The department's morale was low, as was its productivity. Only its levels of errors and absenteeism were high.

Mark quickly made many beneficial changes. He developed a vision for the department and shared it with the group; he developed specific productivity targets; he identified critical values such as quality, customer service, and recognized people when they demonstrated them; he set up an employee-of-the-month program; he encouraged team members to get together socially after work on Fridays, and brought in pizza to celebrate when targets were met.

Productivity and morale jumped, and errors and absenteeism dropped drastically. Within a few months, however, momentum slowed. Although performance was still higher than before Mark took over, it was considerably lower than it had been during his first three months. After seven months, the group seemed to have plateaued, and Mark's enthusiasm and pep rallies could not bring the group back to the superior level of performance that they had initially demonstrated. Puzzled and somewhat discouraged, Mark looked for help in assessing what was happening.

When Mark's staff were interviewed on their perceptions of

the team's strengths and opportunities for improvement, comments were very similar: "Things are great in a lot of ways. Mark's a nice guy and really enthusiastic. He tries to make things fun and he says thanks which is really important, but in many ways things aren't much different than they were a year ago. Mark's the boss, and he makes the decisions. We aren't asked our input on decisions that affect our jobs. He tells us his ideas and asks us what we think, but we don't see any evidence that our opinions count for much. Most of us don't give much input anymore."

You can't build a team if you don't give people the opportunity to participate productively. Other aspects of leadership are also important, of course. Successful leaders have a focus, they display affirmative values, and they establish clear expectations, but without productive participation a team cannot realize its potential. Its members have no sense of ownership of what the team is in place to do; they have no vitality. Mark had been doing many of the right things, but had missed the critical element of productive participation.

The effective leader understands how to ensure productive participation. When members participate productively, their activities produce results. Individuals know their comments are valued, and they become committed. The how-to's of productive participation are discussed in Chapters 2, 3, and 4.

Many leaders who are participative at heart are not participative in action. The flexible leader periodically assesses to what extent she puts her commitment to participation into action.

Leadership Dimension 4: Challenging Others

Mediocrity does not exist in a fit team. The superior team is consistently challenged to attain greater heights. For the most part, this is because the leader of the fit team knows how to create challenges that can't be ignored.

An irresistible challenge is one that stretches team members so that they feel a sense of accomplishment. It does not, however, set discouragingly high goals which may appear nearly unattainable. An irresistible challenge offers an opportunity for growth. It may create an opportunity to try something new or to try out skills and aptitudes perhaps not used on a daily basis. An irresistible challenge includes built-in rewards. An irresistible challenge is described in such a way that meeting it becomes an expectation in the minds of team members (as discussed in Leadership Dimension 3: Focusing with Feeling). An irresistible challenge is either relatively quickly met or has built-in measurements to ensure a sense of accomplishment along the way.

Not every challenge that effectively motivates meets each of these criteria, but it generally meets several. Challenges take two forms. Team challenges, which all team members work together toward, and individual challenges. Both are important.

If team members' daily tasks have become routine and mundane, they are probably not performing at a high level. Each team member needs to feel that the piece of the team puzzle for which she is responsible is important and that she is doing something in which she can take pride. If members are to have renewed bursts of energy, essential to high performance, they must be challenged.

Effective delegation is one of the simplest means of challenging. If a manager treats delegating as a means of getting rid of the tedious chores for which she does not have sufficient time, it will probably be referred to in her group as dumping. If team members are to be challenged through the process of delegation, at least some of the tasks delegated must somehow be enriching. Some of the tasks delegated must stretch the individual. They may provide opportunity for exposure in the organization, they may provide variety, or an opportunity to hone skills. To check whether you challenge through delegation, ask yourself:

- Am I holding on to any task which members of my team could be competently carrying out?
- Am I preparing people through development to take on more responsibility?

• Do I look for an opportunity to delegate "interesting" tasks?

Tasks are most challenging when the individual is allowed to operate independently. The traditional organization creates many checkpoints that are manned by the supervisor. This overseeing prevents any sense of job ownership and the challenge that goes with it. That each member has a sense of job ownership is important to the flexible team. This requires more authority and accountability and fewer management-manned checkpoints. It requires a leader who sees as one of his major tasks that of continuously enriching the job for those reporting to him and enabling them to handle the challenge by providing development and resources when necessary. Challenging, empowering, and enabling are all part of the same leadership dimension. Irresistible team challenges meet the same criteria as effective individual challenges, but on a broader scale.

The challenge created by the leader does not exist only in specific tasks or projects. The challenge to team members to be consistently high performers is clearly and consistently communicated as an expectation of superior leaders. They do not find it necessary to make speeches on performance. Their high expectations are expressed consistently in everything they say and do.

Limp leaders communicate low expectations. Often leaders don't recognize that they are sending limp messages, thereby getting low performance in return.

A team leader had asked individuals to do some research on a particular topic before a meeting and to come prepared to share that information with the group. The individuals had agreed. At the meeting, the leader opened: "It has been a busy couple of weeks. Has anyone had time to get the information together?" His message was clear: "I don't expect that the assignments were completed and it's okay if you don't complete assigned tasks." It wasn't surprising that only one out of six had done anything and that what that one person had done was little more than a gesture of compliance.

In this case, the likelihood of team members having produced something would have been much higher if they had expected to hear and had heard, "What have you got for us?" They came unprepared because their leader consistently sent the message that it was okay not to fulfill commitments. If a leader consistently sends messages that affirm his expectations, most team members will live up to them.

Effective leaders create challenging environments by constantly and consistently communicating high expectations and by providing abundant opportunities for team members to display their skills.

Workouts for Developing Leadership Strength

Workout: To assess your organizational fit.

Steps: Check off those statements that describe your situation.

I enjoy my leadership role.	☐
I feel confident in handling it.	☐
I see potential problems as challenges.	☐
I make decisions easily.	☐
Team members are challenged by me but are also comfortable with me.	☐
I have personally clarified my beliefs about the team and its priorities and demonstrate them consistently.	☐

If these statements for the most part describe you, you are probably a centered leader who feels professionally confident and comfortable. Your sense of professional well-being is felt by the people around you, and they respond with the desire to emulate your professional centeredness and a desire to follow where you lead.

Workout: To assess your organizational fit.

Steps: Rate each of the following statements as to the extent to which it describes your situation.

1 not at all
2 somewhat
3 to a great extent
4 completely

1. I agree with organizational decisions that I have to introduce.

    1 2 3 4

2. I feel I can control the future of my team.

    1 2 3 4

3. I feel my concerns and suggestions are listened to and when possible acted upon.

    1 2 3 4

4. I look forward to coming to work in the morning.

    1 2 3 4

5. I know where the organization is going.

    1 2 3 4

6. I am comfortable with the direction the organization is taking.

    1 2 3 4

7. I feel senior management's priorities are appropriate.

    1 2 3 4

8. I like the way people are treated in this organization.

    1 2 3 4

If you have rated six or more statements a three or four, you probably have a comfortable organizational fit. If the statements for the most part do not describe your situation (i.e., you have many ones and twos), you are very much out of sync with your organization. If this is the case, consider the following:

1. Have you made active attempts to lessen the disparity between your organization and yourself? (That is, have you expressed your concerns to the *right* people in a positive manner?)

Yes _____ No _____

2. If no, what steps might you take?

_____

_____

_____

3. If you see little chance of lessening the difference between yourself and your organization, can you personally change your attitude toward the situation sufficiently to allow you to be a committed leader?

Yes _____ No _____

4. If yes, specifically what will you do?

_____

_____

_____

(Check regularly to ensure that you are consistently living up to these personal commitments.)

5. If no, what career alternatives do you have?

_____

_____

_____

Managers who suffer from lethargy or fear of change tend to accept things as they are. The unpleasant known is somehow better to them than a potentially brighter unknown that requires effort and risk. They shrug and ask, "What can I do about it?" not expecting or wanting any productive responses. They resign themselves and their teams to mediocrity.

Workout: To test your leadership beliefs.

Steps: Rate yourself as honestly as possible on the four-point scale.

1 This is not true at all.
2 This is true some of the time.
3 This is true most of the time.
4 This is true consistently.

Better still, ask the members of a team you lead to rate you.

1. I involve people in the decisions that affect them.
   1 2 3 4
2. I keep people well informed.
   1 2 3 4
3. I frequently receive ideas and suggestions from the people I lead.
   1 2 3 4
4. I consider employees' ideas with an open mind.
   1 2 3 4
5. I implement employees' ideas whenever possible.
   1 2 3 4
6. I expect team members for the most part to make their own decisions on how their job will be done.
   1 2 3 4
7. I look for opportunities to give my team members challenging and interesting responsibilities.
   1 2 3 4
8. I am open to receiving comments from team members on how I can do things more effectively.
   1 2 3 4
9. I increase team members' responsibility and authority whenever possible.
   1 2 3 4

Total the numbers you have circled. Your score will range between nine and thirty-six. The higher your score, the more closely you are aligned to the beliefs and behaviors of managers who lead superior teams.

Workout: To identify opportunities for empowering members of your team.

Steps:
1. Choose a team member who reports to you. Develop a list of major tasks which this individual is responsible for and categorize them as follows:
    i) is completely responsible, does not need to see me on these items;
    ii) can make a decision independently, but must keep me posted;
    iii) must check with me before acting on these items.
2. Have the team member complete her own list and categorize it.
3. Compare notes.
4. Are there opportunities for moving a (iii) to a (ii), or a (ii) to a (i)?

11

Self-Managed Work Teams

The epitome of teamwork is the self-managed work team. It is the ultimate demonstration of team fitness.

Self-managed teams are a natural outcome of the evolution of the flexible organization. As we move to create leaner, flatter organizations with fewer management levels, foster ownership by passing down more authority and decision-making power, and build teams, we simultaneously decrease the amount of supervision required.

In some instances, self-managed teams evolve as a result of a team and its leader consciously working on team development, but with no intent of creating a self-managed team. In one situation, as team members increased their ability to work together, to solve problems, and to make their own decisions, the supervisor found that she had more time to become involved in other activities outside of her unit. She spent more and more time away, and as the team continued to develop, she and the members realized that the team could indeed manage on its own. This is not a common scenario. In most organizations that boast self-managed work teams, teams have been carefully developed, and they have specific objectives: fulfilled and committed employees, increased quality, productivity, and cost savings.

These self-directed groups are still relatively rare and are more prevalent on the shop floor than in the office. Many teams that are considered self-managed are assigned an individual who is responsible for providing some supervisory support. This individual, who may coordinate several groups, is likely to assist them in their development and problem solving, act as an advisor on work-related issues, and play a management role in decision-making, when required. The coordinator may be the decision-maker if the group does not have the skills, information, or experience required to make a decision or if the urgency of the problem renders it inappropriate for group decision-making.

Self-managed teams, which are literally self-managed and do not have a coordinator, are not left to work in a vacuum. They normally have a facilitator, well skilled in team development and group process, who meets with them regularly to support them in continued development, in critiquing their performance, in resolving conflict, and in problem solving.

When individuals responsible for the development of self-managed work teams were asked what they believed were the critical criteria for success, they cited the following:

A Champion to Maintain Management Commitment
A deep conviction that the work world would indeed be better for all concerned if teams were able to function without direct supervision was high on the list of musts. A champion was considered essential to maintain management commitment when the going gets rough, as it often does.

Management had to recognize that the development of these teams would take time and had to be sufficiently committed to grant the time and budget required.

Training and Team Development
On occasion, groups have been empowered without being given the proper tools for performance. Most organizations now recognize the need for leadership training. Not all recognize the need for team membership training which is critical, of course, if the team is to manage itself. This includes meeting management, group decision-making, the resolution of conflict, team building, and basic management.

Understanding Why
Groups designated for self-management develop much more quickly if time is spent sharing the organizational vision and

how the self-managed work team fits into that vision. If they understand why their organization is moving toward self-management, they can appreciate the benefits, and development is accelerated. When this information is not shared, the management motive is often suspect and resistance to the process results.

Clear Guidelines and Parameters of Authority

In one administrative area, a self-managed team that erupted rather than evolving or consciously developing experienced serious difficulties because management hadn't preplanned. The group found itself managing without having answers to important basic questions, such as: Who appraises our performance? Are we still appraised individually or as a team? What authority do we have? Do we have a budget? How do we link to management?

Time must be taken to work through all guidelines and parameters of authority carefully with the new self-managed work team. This discussion is a prerequisite in that it provides the information required to manage, but in addition the process is often an important support for a new work team, which may not as yet be fully confident.

Realistic Expectations

Unless a great deal of team development has gone before, self-managed teams don't happen overnight. Some groups lend themselves more readily to self-management than others. Fit teams that are flexible are ripe for self-management. Rigid or limp groups need a good deal of development.

Some groups do not have the aptitude for self-management. Although they can usually develop some degree of increased self-direction, it may be minimal. This ineligibility for self-management should be evident early on in the process. The reality is that some groups become viable candidates only after the membership of the group changes.

However, if groups are screened for their potential before development actually begins, opportunities are sometimes missed. Some groups who have previously shown little incentive, commitment, or teamwork potential, suddenly come alive when challenged and given teamwork tools.

Rather than designating that certain groups become self-managed teams, the ideal is to have all teams embarking on team development. Some groups will plateau early, of these some will continue to require full-time supervision, others part-time. The fittest groups will attain self-management.

Not only are self-managed teams a natural step in the evolution of the modern participative organization, but they will become an even more necessary step. As our organizations become increasingly knowledge-based and made up of specialists who are self-directed with input from colleagues and others, self-managed teams will continue to grow in number.

In 1988, Peter Drucker predicted that within twenty years the typical large business would have fewer than half the levels of management of its 1988 counterpart and no more than a third of its managers.

The management fear of "What will happen to me once the team can function without a leader?" has caused some managers to resist the process. It is going to be impossible to resist. Managers who excel in their organizations will be those who welcome the opportunity to develop their teams, have the skills to foster ownership and self-direction in those reporting to them, can effectively manage change through the team process, and can function effectively themselves as a management team member.

12

Making Committees Work

When a committee works well, it is the epitome of what teamwork is all about. Diversified experience, ideas, and points of view interact dynamically to create the best possible outcome. The committee's activity and results are exciting and productive. They generate waves of energy which move out into the organization, sparking renewed commitment and superior accomplishments.

Every new committee that is struck holds this potential. A much smaller portion than we would like actually realizes it. Many organizations, in fact, see committees as more of a necessary evil than a superior method of getting things done.

Organizations choose to establish a committee for a variety of reasons. Management may recognize a need to get people involved, whether to meet employee demands and expectations, to get their ideas, to have a cross-fertilization of ideas, or to develop a sense of ownership. Sometimes a committee is put in place to get a job done that is outside of any particular departmental mandate. Committees are becoming more and more a way of organizational life, but they can be a very costly method in terms of the use of human resources. It makes sense, then, that these committees and task forces be used effectively.

Often committees have a much tougher time than need be because potential challenges aren't recognized in the planning stage. In the worst possible scenario, no planning stage exists. Management assumes that if a few half-willing bodies are mixed together and little luck is added that something worthwhile will result.

Getting Started

Slow starts aren't unusual. Committees are most frequently made up of representatives from various functions across an organization. Most have likely not worked together before, some have not even met each other before. Their working styles may be very different. Some may have a very vague notion of why they are there. Others may have been assigned to the committee and don't want to be there. Some come bearing their personal or departmental priorities and biases. Yet we often expect that with no direct intervention, this collection of individuals will quickly cohere and efficiently and effectively produce results.

The tension of slow starts can further impede the process. When progress isn't forthcoming as quickly as expected, management starts prodding and probing. When coworkers who are carrying an extra workload for committee members see nothing coming out of meetings, their reaction is less than supportive. Supervisors, who run short-staffed during meetings and were probably unhappy about it to begin with, have difficulty smiling a sincere smile and saying "great" when the employee reminds her she'll be away for a couple of hours at a meeting. When that meeting appears to produce little, committee members themselves feel frustrated, and this feeling is compounded by critical or unsupportive responses from those around them. The morale of the committee drops, and the group has even greater difficulty in becoming productive. The speed with which a group becomes functional is in direct proportion to a) the clarity of its mandate and of management's expectations; and b) the speed with which a team is effectively developed.

Management's Responsibilities

Although it is the committee that is ultimately successful or unsuccessful, the foundation that management lays to a great extent determines the degree to which the committee succeeds.

Many false starts and not-so-successful stories could have been prevented if management had provided the essentials to do the job.

A clearly defined mandate is critical to a committee's success. On the surface, this criterion for success appears obvious, yet it is frequently not fulfilled. The mandate should act as a beacon for committees; it should give the group a clear picture of where it needs to go. It should act as a focal point and a reminder of the group's responsibility. Many of the committees and task forces that mushroomed during the management drive to develop new, more participative cultures have too-broad or unclear mandates. Committees such as employee-involvement groups, quality task forces, and customer-service committees often have very broad mandates: for example, "To introduce programs to enhance the Better Manufacturing Company's customer service." Mandates such as this, with no specific goals, objectives, or expectations tied to them have a slim chance of acting as a beacon.

Management also needs to provide committee members with the parameters of their task, itemizing anything that may be off-limits; with the criteria management will use to judge the project or make a final decision; with any information that management holds that is critical to determining the best recommendations or decisions; and with a clear picture of the committee's role and the level at which it is invited to participate in the decision-making process.

A manufacturing company, which wanted to increase employee participation, established a space-evaluation committee whose mandate was "To develop a plan to utilize the front office space most effectively." The committee was motivated. Most of the individuals had worked together before. They all came to the initial meeting with ideas. Each was committed and followed through on any task assigned to be done between committee meetings. As a result, in a short time they had put together a detailed plan and enthusiastically presented it to the management group. The management group responded, "Well done, but . . ."

After the *but*, the management group redesigned the plan. Some changes were based on personal views such as, "I think it would be much more attractive to have the library corner with the periodicals by the window." Other comments were based on a criterion that was important to the president, but hadn't been shared with the committee: "The president has decided that he wants closer contact with customer service and finance so they should be at his end of the office." Some changes were the result of information the committee didn't have: "We're adding three people in accounting. You need more space in that department."

The committee went away, somewhat let down and frustrated, to rework the plan.

On the next presentation, the management group again asked for significant changes. The committee was left with the impression that its participation was only tokenism. "If management already knew what they wanted, why waste our time?"

Members found excuses not to attend meetings. In the end, a few team members halfheartedly put together a final draft and turned it over to management. This unsuccessful attempt at participation had damaging short- and long-term consequences. In the short term, a good deal of time was wasted, and morale was damaged. Long-term damage included distrust and cynicism on the part of committee members and close observers. The next management effort to establish a committee was met with distrust and resistance.

Forming a committee, then, like any other implementation of change in an organization, requires some preplanning on the part of management. Committees don't just happen or at least not effectively. In the management-planning stage, each of these essentials must be considered:

Clarity of mandate. Will committee members understand exactly what their role is? The mandate of the group in the above case stated: "To develop a plan to utilize the front office space most effectively." Management did not state at which level of participation in the decision-making process they were asking the committee to function (Chapter 2). They did not explain whether they expected members to bring information and ideas to the decision-making process (Level III) or whether they were to function at Level II, which would be actually sharing the decision-making. If functioning at Level III, the committee might simply draw up a rough draft of ideas which the management group would then use to develop the final plan and to make its decision. Functioning at Level II, the committee would be expected to produce a carefully researched and fully developed plan which management would anticipate being able to implement basically as presented. Since management hadn't clarified its expectations, the committee members assumed that they were being empowered to make a recommendation that in all likelihood would be accepted with a few minor changes. The time invested in attempting to develop and polish a finished product was much greater, of course, than would have been required to develop a rough draft for the management group to use.

Decision-making criteria. If a recommendation is to be brought to management for a decision as a result of a committee's work, management must determine the criteria it will use to make that decision and must decide if it is prepared to share that criteria with the committee. In the example we have been using, one criterion was that finance and customer service be in close proximity to the president's office.

Pertinent information. Management must ensure that the committee has all information necessary to fulfill its mandate at the outset and that members are updated as any new information comes along. In our example, the addition of three people to accounts receivable was important information which the committee did not hold.

Management's role. Has the management group clarified its own role in the decision-making process? If, for example, the committee is empowered to present a plan which is expected to be implemented and if the committee has been provided with the required information and criteria, management's role should simply be to evaluate the recommendation against the criteria.

Selecting Committee Members

Managers recognize the need to have the right person in the right job, and they spend time checking that skills and aptitudes match the job requirements.

Committees are fulfilling important functions. (If not, their existence should be questioned.) Yet, we often see little thought given to selecting the right people for a committee. Whether a committee is appointed or is a volunteer group, a list of criteria can facilitate the selection process and enhance the results. Often appointed members are chosen for the wrong reasons. Someone may decide that Departments A, B, C, and D should send representatives. The departments' supervisors then choose individuals to sit on the committee. However, too often no specific criteria as to qualities and skills are given. A committee member may then be chosen for any number of reasons. She may be chosen because she has a light workload; because she is most likely to say yes; or because the supervisor is pleased with the individual's work and sees appointment to the committee as a perk. Appointees may be on a committee because they believe it would be politically unsound to reject the appointment, but have little interest in the purpose of the committee.

Volunteer committees that don't stipulate clear criteria for membership frequently end up with individuals who are there for their own reasons. When sufficient volunteers aren't forthcoming, the common scenario is that anyone who can be talked into saying yes becomes a prime candidate.

Selection criteria will vary according to the role the committee is to fulfill and the skills required to fulfill that role. Not only does the use of selection criteria help ensure that the right people are on the committee, but it also establishes that the committee is serious business. High standards and expectations are laid down at the beginning.

The completion of an application form emphasizes to candidates the importance of the committee. The application or proposal form and the selection criteria can be combined, as illustrated in the following sample.

Proposed Membership to the Customer Service Committee

Each individual selected to the Customer Service Committee must meet the following criteria.

Please give evidence where required when a response is Yes.

Name of Candidate: _____

	Yes	No
1. Has a demonstrated belief in quality customer service. **Evidence:**		
2. Has a particular strength in at least one of the following areas: i) Creating Ideas **Evidence:** ii) Gaining Sponsorship for Ideas **Evidence:** iii) Facilitating Groups **Evidence:** iv) Managing Projects **Evidence:**		

v) Presentation Skills

Evidence:

3. Is willing and able to meet for two hours every other week.

4. Has at least four hours per month available for committee work outside of meetings.

5. Has a desire to be on the committee.

Developing Teamwork

Committees, in their urgency to accomplish, frequently "dive right in" and begin work on fulfilling their mandates in their first meetings. Too-quick beginnings often lead to very slow finishes. The disparate personalities, priorities, motives, and understandings brought to committees make it very difficult to make headway without some team development and planning. "We don't have time!" the task-oriented members protest when a team-development session is suggested.

Individuals who have experienced working on committees that have done early development and on those that haven't know that a committee does not have time not to. The team-development session can appear time consuming beforehand, but it definitely saves time in the long run and dramatically increases the level of success achieved.

Some individuals resist team development because they see it as focused purely on process and on relationships. Indeed, in the past, it has often been just that. However, the most effective team development for committees is task focused. In essence, a very productive planning process is combined with team-development workouts.

The length of time devoted varies from half a day to two or three days, depending on the makeup of the committee, the magnitude of the mandate, and of course, the reality that we must all deal with — time available. The session is most effectively facilitated by someone from outside the committee so that all committee members may fully participate.

The following are topics which might be included on a team-development-and-planning agenda:

Clarifying the Mandate

A mandate can be accepted by a committee or it can be *owned* by its members. A simple opportunity for discussing the mandate in a structured forum greatly increases the likelihood of ownership.

We find that when team development is working at its best, the focus is on an aspect of the task at hand, but the resulting benefits go far beyond this specific task. This is the case when a committee's mandate is effectively discussed. The task at hand is the clarification of the mandate to ensure a common interpretation. The additional and equally important outcome is that by the end of the discussion, the members have made it their own. What they had previously agreed to, they are now excited about, and the level of commitment soars.

This discussion session normally verifies everyone's understanding of the mandate. On the surface, the mandate may appear to be self-explanatory, and the group may suggest "We know what it is; we don't need to spend time on it." But facilitators need to investigate that understanding before they acquiesce to the group's suggestion.

We previously used the statement "To develop programs to enhance customer service" as an example of a mandate. In this case, committee members thought the mandate was self-explanatory because they assumed that they all interpreted it in the same way. When they started looking at it in more detail, however, they found considerable disagreement on what was meant by "programs," "enhance," and even what "customer service" included. They eventually had to go back to management for clarification.

That all members understand and agree on what they have been put in place to do is obviously important. What is not so obvious is that a lack of understanding of aspects of the mandate most frequently bogs a committee down. When a group can't come to agreement, it is often because some aspect of the mandate or criterion relating to it has been interpreted inconsistently. In the case of this committee, members likely would have had a good deal of difficulty in coming to consensus on which programs to choose since they each had a different interpretation of what "program" meant.

A group usually does not realize that the root of its disagreement is varying interpretations of the mandate. When it does become apparent, members are shocked to recognize that they have been working for weeks, even months, using quite different interpretations. "No wonder," groaned a committee member whose group just recognized its dilemma, "we seemed to be working at cross-purposes, and it has been so damn frustrating!"

When a committee clarifies its mandate, it may find that a consistent understanding is indeed in place, but the time taken to make sure is worthwhile.

Defining the Ground Rules

This important element of teamwork was discussed in Chapter 6. By establishing ground rules, team members have an opportunity to clarify and express their expectations of each other. Some ground rules may apply to committee meetings while others may apply to members' behavior and actions as they relate to committee work outside of actual meetings.

If the list of ground rules becomes too lengthy, none of the rules is likely to make much of an impact. Some groups opt for two different sets of considerations and a separate discussion on each: ground rules for committee meetings; and team members' responsibilities. This division provides more structure and focus. Ground rules for committee meetings often include the obvious:

- to arrive on time for all meetings;
- to respect each others' opinion;
- to participate in meetings.

Committees can easily end up with a collection of motherhood statements to which everyone nods in agreement. Ground rules should be based on observable and preferably measurable behavior. In all likelihood, many ground rules presented by members will not meet this criterion. Members must probe for, clarify, and document observable behavior to support a ground rule. For example, if "to respect each other's opinion" is to be used a ground rule, committee members must be able to agree upon what "respect" means in terms of behavior. If this ground rule is to be a useful tool, members will need to discuss "What behaviors would indicate that we are not respecting each other's opinions?" Responses might be: "When we shoot down someone's idea" or "when we cut someone off." Or one might ask: "What behaviors would indicate that we *are* respecting each other's opinions?"

Meeting ground rules are usually, on the surface, fairly basic. When more senior employees are doing team development, they often feel that "We are experienced enough in meetings. We don't need that." And sometimes they don't. On occasion, however, when a senior manager has had the insight and courage to respond "I'm not so sure about that," the resulting discussion and ground rules have made a difference.

Meetings of senior management personnel often have many of the same destructive characteristics as meetings of junior-level staff. People jump on each other's ideas, don't listen, arrive late, come unprepared, and so on.

Developing ground rules sometimes seems too basic because what we list is what we already know we should do. Its usefulness is in reminding us of what is and is not okay, and in establishing standards which the team expects all of its members to live up to. Once these standards have been expressed, appropriate behavior is more likely to be forthcoming.

Developing ground rules also gives members permission to address related issues. In one task force on quality, a member was frustrated that other members didn't come to meetings prepared and as a result considerable time was being wasted. He was hesitant, however, to raise his concerns. If the ground rule had been established that everyone come prepared, the individual could have more comfortably addressed the issue by saying, "We agreed in the beginning that we would all come prepared, and I haven't seen that happening."

Success Requirements

Essential to an effective team-development-and-planning session is a look at what we have to do to get where we want to go.

Once the committee has clarified its mandate, it has a definition of success. Success Requirements, then, are the areas the team must focus on to meet with that success. An employee-involvement committee listed three of its SR's as:

- keeping all employees aware of what we are doing;
- having an effective line of communication with management;
- having enough time.

Most groups identify six to eight critical success requirements. Then, the team discusses and comes to agreement on specific strategies for fulfilling each of the SR's. Critical success requirements, when reviewed on a regular basis, ensure that priority areas receive the attention required. A review of the SR's can also ensure that committees do not spend more time than appropriate on areas of less importance. The best return on investment from the committee's team-development-and-planning session occurs when the results of the session are periodically used to check progress and direction. Committee members leave well-facilitated team-development sessions with a high level of commitment, clear direction, and a plan of action.

Workouts for Developing Effective Committees

Material that lends itself to workouts for committees has been incorporated throughout Chapter 12.

Workout: To establish an effective committee.

Steps: Committee organizers check whether all essentials described on pages 160-62 have been met.

- Is the committee's mandate clear?
- Are management decision-making criteria clear and shared with the committee?
- Have we identified what information is important to the committee to enable them to do their job well and are we prepared to share it?
- Have we established criteria for eligibility for committee membership?

Workout: To develop the committee as a team.

Steps: Conduct a focusing and team-development session. The agenda might include:
- clarifying the mandate;
- defining the ground rules;
- identifying Success Requirements;
- making commitments to action to ensure SR's are met.
Details are provided on pages 168-69.

13

Common Teamwork Questions

Assimilating the New Team Member

Getting a new team member up and running and part of the team quickly is often a challenge for a leader. A critical factor is, of course, identifying the right person in the first place. Whether the new member fits is often nothing more than luck.

"The same people had been working together as a team for some time," explained a nursing-team manager. "We decided we needed some new blood. We made an effort to bring in someone new with fresh and different ideas, but it just didn't work. She didn't fit."

The team had taken a big step in recognizing the need for "new blood" and in bringing someone new into the group. Their problem, however, was that they had no means of testing the new member's blood type. She wasn't a match.

Determining whether someone is a match for a work group is usually hit and miss. If the resume and references are good, she presents herself professionally, and the manager is comfortable with her, we hire her and keep our fingers crossed.

The new team member is taking a risk as well. A job description, however appealing, gives the candidate little indication of whether the seven or eight hours a day that she will spend in the new workplace will be a good experience. The way the team works will ultimately determine the level of satisfaction rather than what the team does.

One of the advantages of team development is that it makes matching the right person with the right team easier. When a group doesn't know who it is, how can it know what characteristics are required of someone new? As the group develops cohesiveness and identity through a team-development process and identifies what is important to it and what its priorities are, describing the ideal team member is easier. Assisting candidates in identifying if this team is right for them is also easier.

In undeveloped teams, a good deal of time is wasted as the new member feels his way, checking out what's okay and what's not. Team members meanwhile observe and size up the new member, consciously or unconsciously deciding whether he is fit and whether he will be accepted fully.

The integration process is speeded up when the team's work values, priorities, and ground rules are shared with the new team member and discussed in a team meeting. This allows team members an opportunity to share their perspectives on why a particular value or ground rule is important and to give examples of how it is demonstrated and fulfilled.

An important element in the success of the session is a clarification that, although this is the way the team believes it needs to work if it is to reach its optimum potential, it welcomes new ideas. Once again, that challenge of balance is critical. The team believes it has found some of the right answers and so requests that new team members conform to the team's culture. Yet at one and the same time, the team must remain open, welcome new ideas, and be receptive to appropriate changes.

The process of sharing and discussing values and ground rules with the new team member not only puts him in the cultural picture quickly, but also reenergizes all team members, as the sharing of one's beliefs with others so often does.

Finally, new team members are most quickly integrated when they are quickly involved. New team members are often left to sit on the periphery for a while on the assumption that they need time to get a feel for what is done and how. The speed of a new member's assimilation, however, is most often in direct proportion to his degree of involvement. Let him get involved in group decision-making, projects, task forces, or whatever else may be happening as quickly as possible.

What Do You Do with the Non-Team Player?

Not everyone fits easily into a teamwork process. Some people simply prefer working independently or do not enjoy sharing or being involved in group processes. The rigid individual, who requires a good deal of structure, may have very definite ideas on how things should be done and may not be receptive to compromise.

How to get non-team players on board is a frequent frustration for team leaders and members. How teams normally contend with non-team players is not unlike how the human body deals with foreign particles. If a small foreign particle, such as a sliver, enters the human body, the body usually deals with it by rejecting it or encapsulating or isolating it in order to protect the rest of the body from the particle. This guards the body against irritation and possibly infection. What happens with a non-team player is often quite similar.

Rejection

Once a group consistently demonstrates that it believes in the team process, the non-team player often opts to move elsewhere. The solution is not, however, always that simple. The non-team player may feel she is too close to retirement to change or may fear change. If teamwork and participation are clearly part of performance requirements, the leader may initiate the removal of the individual, or a transfer to any area that allows more independent work.

Isolating the Non-Team Player

A well-developed team often isolates a non-team player with no malice or harm to the esteem of this member. This behavior is evident in the following example of an accounting-group's team-building workshop.

Diane had participated when asked, but not spontaneously during the morning session. She frequently disappeared and would reappear after fifteen or twenty minutes. Some team members assumed that she was taking a smoke break. However, Diane disappeared in the early afternoon and never returned. Team members shrugged. "That's Diane," they commented. "She doesn't like teamwork, but she's a darn good computer operator."

The group had recognized that Diane didn't fit into the team and probably never would. They recognized that even though she was not participative, she did contribute in her own way to the team's success. They realized that because of the way their organization worked, management was unlikely to remove any team member. Although they realized that the team would be even better if everyone were a fully participating member, they accepted the fact that this was not their reality and were determined not to allow that fact to deter the rest of them from working as a team.

They were in fact isolating or encapsulating Diane. They were not in anyway ostracizing her — they accepted her as she was — but at the same time they would not allow her to infect the rest of the team.

In most cases, team members do not discuss this behavior — they may not even recognize it — they just do it.

Changing Shape

What perhaps happens most frequently is that the non-team player subtly changes shape over time. He or she may not be a perfect fit, but the sharp points which cause the most irritation are somewhat rounded off. This happens as the non-team member conforms to some extent to the established team norms and to the expectations of the leader and the team.

This change happens only when expectations are clear and consistent. Providing the non-team member is not resisting solely for the sake of resisting, she will usually make an effort to conform to as great an extent as is possible for her. Most individuals make an attempt to meet others' expectations.

△ — rigid non-team players

○ — flexible team players

△ — Changing Shape

How Do You Get Non-Participative Members To Participate?

In some cases, a non-participative member is the non-team player described above. In other cases, however, he is an individual who is not confident about participating in a group and so often contributes little or nothing. Or he may be someone who feels no responsibility for contributing.

Once again, clear expectations are vital. Members must communicate that participation is not just an opportunity, but a responsibility, and that people are being invited to participate not just for participation's sake, but because their input is valued, needed, and will be used. Hesitancy to participate occurs most often in groups that are undeveloped and have seldom had the opportunity to participate. When this is the case, the facilitator may structure the process in such a way as to make participation easy.

A tool that has been around for a long time, but is still useful is the Nominal Group Technique. (This technique has many other names.) Most people who have been involved in a group process have used it or will recognize it, and anyone who has participated in a brainstorming session will recognize at least a part of it. Several versions exist, but it usually follows this format. Once the topic which requires input and ideas has been described, the facilitator leads the group through:

- Silent Generation of Ideas
- Round-Robin Sharing and Recording of Ideas
- Discussion of Each Recorded Idea
- Identifying Priorities
- Final Decision and Checking for Consensus.

The most productive step of all and the one most often ignored is the first — the silent generation of ideas. This step has several benefits when a facilitator requires input.

Often individuals run to a meeting with their minds still on the activity they have just left. When the facilitator asks for ideas on a particular topic, especially with a relatively undeveloped group, one of two things often happens. One or two people immediately jump in with ideas. These are the group members who enjoy the participation process, think well out loud, and need no encouragement. Or a silence settles upon the group. The silence may in reality be quite short, but in North America we tend to be uncomfortable with dead air and if the leader is not a skilled facilitator, he usually jumps in himself with, "Well, I was thinking," hoping to get things started. In both cases, only one or two team members participate in the fullest sense. While other members may contribute to the discussion, their participation is often a reaction to the ideas already presented rather than the development of their own ideas.

A time for the silent generation of ideas helps ensure that everyone is taking responsibility for developing ideas. It does so by giving everyone time to set aside what was happening just before he or she came into the meeting and to get himself or herself into the discussion at hand. It also helps individuals who are strong at developing ideas as well as those who are less spontaneous and who develop ideas most effectively in a quiet environment. This is often a trait of the non-participative team member.

A time for the silent generation of ideas usually takes only a few minutes and is well invested. If a useful agenda which allows people to prepare for a meeting is circulated, and if it is the norm for people to come prepared, this step may not be necessary. But it is important to give people at least enough time to collect their thoughts.

The round-robin step in which ideas are collected, one idea per person until all ideas are drained, ensures that *everyone* contributes the idea that he or she has jotted down. A ground rule stating that ideas are not discussed at this point prevents any evaluation and helps to protect the less confident participant.

When a process such as this one is used regularly, the expectation that everyone will participate is clearly communicated. In the beginning, the non-participative member may pass, but if this becomes the normal way of doing things and most people are participating, he or she usually begins to make some effort to conform and to share ideas. For some non-participative members, it takes proof that the participation is risk free (see Chapter 6) and that it will produce a result. When these elements are present, non-participants usually become increasingly involved.

Some people will always be more participative than others. Leaders frequently ask, "How do we get equal participation"? To expect everyone to want and use equal air time, however, is unrealistic. But we can and will get to the point where everyone sees developing ideas, giving input, and sharing problem-solving and decision-making as an integral part of his or her job.

Achieving participation is much less of a challenge than it was five to ten years ago. It is unlikely that it will even be raised as a concern ten years from now. Two major factors will contribute to this. First, participation will be the norm. For most employees who will have been in the work force for fifteen years or less, it will simply be the way things have always been done. For older employees, ten years will give them time to adjust or retire.

Second, the adaptation of the new employee to a participative environment is also being made easier by the fact that the environment in most schools has become consultative. As early as grade one, students are being trained to work independently, to make their own decisions about how and in what order they get their assignments done, and to approach the teacher for consultation when support is needed. Training is being given on how to share, how to work in teams, and how to support team members.

The result of these two factors is already being felt in our most progressive corporations.

The future of teamwork and participation are exciting. When they become a natural part of the way we work and people enter the work force with teamwork skills already in place, groups will realize their potential quickly and with a great deal more ease.

Fit Teams — Ready for a Decade of Improvement

And so, what does all of this mean for the leader, the human-resource specialist, and the organization?

It means that the organizations that will thrive are giving up the frenetic and exhausting search for excellence because they recognize that they have found the success ingredients they need. They just have to apply them.

It means they are giving up the buzz words that have no sting and have too often become a drone and instead of inspiring people have put them to sleep.

It means we can stop flitting from one trendy program to the next in fear that we may be missing the "answer" or the improved ingredient that will guarantee excellence. (How many programs has your organization sampled over the past ten years and how many are still in place or have produced lasting results?)

It means we can stop looking for eureka. We can stop worrying whether we've put our money and time into the "best" program or whether an even better one is around the corner. We can relax, take a deep breath, and focus on developing fit teams, knowing that they will be as relevant ten years from now as they are today. We can relax, knowing that when issues of service, quality, or productivity arise, they can be handled for the most part within the context of the teams responsible, without launching glitzy new and expensive programs.

What needs to be done is fairly simple and straightforward. We have to develop and maintain fit teams: groups with strong cohesiveness, openness, participative ability, group skills, and change compatibility. How we develop these elements in our organization is not quite as simple, but neither is it difficult. It is a matter of avoiding the North American organizational Achilles' heel of not applying what we know. It is a matter of taking time to identify which elements need strengthening and going through the workouts required to develop them. The workouts you choose may be some of those described in the past chapters, or your team may work out simply by assessing what needs to be done differently, making specific commitments, and doing it.

Excuses that look like good reasons for not beginning and sticking to a team-fitness program are easy to find. Don't let the waylayers sidetrack you.

Waylayers
- *We don't have time.* You don't have time not to. Others are making the time and as their fitness develops, they'll soon leave you behind.
- *Good intentions.* An old adage states: "We judge ourselves by our intentions. We judge others by their actions." I have met many managers who see themselves as flexible leaders, but their peers and employees who are reading their actions, not their minds, describe them as limp.
- *Some people just don't want to participate.* Participation in today's organizational world is not just an opportunity, it's a responsibility.
- *People aren't committed enough to develop team fitness.* It's not that people don't want to be committed; they need something worthwhile to be committed to.

Only one thing can turn limpness or rigidity into flexibility, and that is action.

Team Fitness:
Maintaining the Momentum

The following pages are designed to support the development and maintenance of team fitness. Use the **Personal Highlighter**, page 182, to make note of ideas/tools that you would like to have easily accessible for future use.

The **Fitness Development Recap**, pages 183 to 186, when completed, records the team's development opportunities and the progress which resulted from the use of the Team Fitness Test. It is a useful monitoring and maintenance tool.

The **Fitness Development Indicator**, page 187, documents progress toward increased fitness and self-direction.

Personal Highlighter

TOOL/IDEA	PAGE	TARGET TEAM	APPLICATION OPPORTUNITIES*

* An event, meeting or introduction of change which would provide the opportunity for the introduction of the idea or tool.

Fitness Development Recap

To be used with the Team Fitness Test, page 31.

TEAM:

FITNESS ELEMENT: Productive Participation

PRIORITY RATING (from Team Fitness Test):

OUTPUT FROM TEAM DISCUSSION:

- Needs Identified: (e.g., a need might be "We need to be more involved in decisions which affect us.")

- Commitments to Action for Improvement:*

REVIEW DATE:

REVIEW COMMENTS:

* Commitments must be specific, including what will be done by whom and when

TEAM:

FITNESS ELEMENT: Openness

PRIORITY RATING:

OUTPUT FROM TEAM DISCUSSION:

- Needs Identified: (e.g., "We need to learn to deal with conflict more effectively.")

- Commitments to Action for Improvement:

REVIEW DATE:

REVIEW COMMENTS:

TEAM:

FITNESS ELEMENT: Cohesiveness

PRIORITY RATING:

OUTPUT FROM TEAM DISCUSSION:

- Needs Identified: (e.g., "We need to come to agreement on our priorities.")

- Commitments to Action for Improvement:

REVIEW DATE:

REVIEW COMMENTS:

TEAM:

FITNESS ELEMENT: Change Compatibility

PRIORITY RATING:

OUTPUT FROM TEAM DISCUSSION:

- Needs Identified: (e.g., "When we demonstrate resistance to change, we need to more carefully assess the cause.")

- Commitments to Action for Improvement:

REVIEW DATE:

REVIEW COMMENTS:

Fitness Development Indicator

TRADITIONAL GROUP	INCREASED SELF-DIRECTION	FIT TEAM
Rigid		Flexible
Indicators	Evidence of Development	Date
• Participation in Decision Making (giving input to or sharing decision with management)		
• Independent Decision Making (without leader)		
• Opportunities for Self-Management		
• Skills Development • Group Skills e.g., Group problem solving/ decision making • Management Skills e.g., project management planning; management of change		

About the Author

Leslie Bendaly, a leader in the field of teamwork effectiveness, is founder and head of Ortran Associates. The firm is dedicated to supporting organizations in the development of increased teamwork and the management of organizational change. Ortran provides consulting and training services to organizations across Canada including IBM, Esso Petroleum Canada Limited, Bell Canada, government departments and ministries, education and health-care facilities. Leslie Bendaly also publishes Teamwork Essentials, a popular newsletter. She is a sought after keynote speaker and workshop leader.